# British Cinema Now

Edited by

## Martin Auty and Nick Roddick

BFI Publishing

Published in 1985 by the British Film Institute
127 Charing Cross Road, London WC2H 0EA

Designed by Don Hart
Typeset by Lineage, Watford
Printed in Great Britain by Jason Press Ltd. Hertford

**British Library Cataloguing in Publication Data**

British cinema now
   1. Moving-picture industry – Great Britain
   I. Auty, Martyn II. Roddick, Nick
   384′.8′0941   PN1993.5.G7

   ISBN 0-85170-130-2
       0-85170-131-0 Pbk

# Contents

# Acknowledgments

The stills in this book are reproduced by courtesy of the following: Boyd's Co., British Broadcasting Corporation, BBC Enterprises, BFI Production Board, Channel Four Television, Columbia-EMI-Warner, Goldcrest, Granada Television, HandMade Films, ITC Film Distributors, Derek Jarman, National Film Archive, Palace Pictures, Rank Film Distributors, Sight and Sound, Twentieth Century-Fox, United Artists, Virgin Films. Photo credits: Sophie Baker (p. 37), David Bramley (p. 79), Frank Connor (pp. 53 and 153), David Farrell (p. 50), Philipp Goetz (p. 133).

Cartoon on p. 135 copyright © Alan Parker

# Introduction

Of all the catchphrases of British life, 'mustn't grumble' has always seemed the least characteristic. As a nation, we are much given to whingeing – about the weather, the railways, the falling standards of our football, the absence of any standards from our cricket, the collapsing pound... and the vanishing film industry.

As a result, most books about the British cinema begin with an apology of one kind or another – by the writer for bothering to write on the subject at all; or, more usually, by the writer for the awfulness of the subject being written on.

This book is, sadly, no exception, at any rate to start with. The first two chapters (by one of the editors, yet) sketch in a map of the British film scene which, in the aftermath of the Government's almost entirely negative 1985 Films Bill, can scarcely but be a little bleak.

But the book is not otherwise designed as an apology, and the whingeing hopefully stops there. Rather than complain about the failure of the British cinema to be what we might think it ought to be – a financier's cinema, an artist's cinema, a patriotic cinema, a socialist cinema, even a dreamer's cinema – we have asked our writers to look at what there is and how it works.

Unlike a lot of slim volumes on the cinema, British or otherwise, we have approached the thing as both an art form *and* an industry. Indeed, if there is an emphasis, it is on the latter. Capitalism has been built into the cinema from the very start: films emerged in capitalism's heyday and have reflected that ideology's crises; oppositional films have been opposed to the capitalist mode of production or consumption. To study it outside that context, therefore, can only be misleading.

Accordingly, *British Cinema Now* gives comparatively little space to the work of individual film artists. Doubtless, some readers will find this unsatisfactory. Cinema has, after all, crept into the curricula of the Western world's educational system under the alibi of literature. Since literature is the study of authors, cinema has tended to become that too.

This introduction is not the place to argue auteurism – merely to say that there is little of it in this book. The contributions look at the varying contexts of film production – Government policy (or lack of it), finance, production, distribution, ideology (though less of that, perhaps, than is usual in a BFI publication). The writers' standpoints range from the down-to-earth commercialism of Matthew Silverstone's chapter on financing (by far the least whingeing piece in the book) to the oppositional commitment of Sheila Whitaker's chapter on independent film-making.

Above all, this book is an attempt to avoid the twin poles of much (British) film writing, which has veered from the gushingly aesthetic to the snottily dismissive, and to fill the gap in writing on British cinema between history (of which there is plenty) and sociological analysis (of which there is too much).

What is dealt with here is the cinematic process – funding, film-making, film-showing, film-watching. It is a book about a film industry simultaneously renascent and in crisis. Like that industry, it is contradictory and, at times, consciously irritating. And, we hope, readable and informative.

MARTYN AUTY
NICK RODDICK

# 1

# 'If the United States spoke Spanish, we would have a film industry...'

In these two introductory chapters, **Nick Roddick** looks at the background to British film production in the 1980s – constantly declining admissions, a cinema culture which is a colony of Hollywood, a government which is indifferent (if not actively hostile) – and examines the various ways in which British films are made on the eve of the grandiosely titled 'British Film Year'.

Given the nature of film production – it is not a small-scale, artisanal activity requiring only a genius and a garret, but a complex industrial process dependent on substantial long-term investment, extensive plant and a complicated marketing and distribution system – there have tended to be only two real models for the making of feature films: the American one and the subsidised one. The American studio model, firmly implanted for three-quarters of a century, is a paradigm of capitalist organisation: a factory system, integrating large-scale production, distribution and exhibition, with a massive number of domestic outlets for its products, and a highly developed penetration of the export market. Hollywood has, like all major industries, survived because it has proved to be adaptable to a changing economic climate. But the prerequisite for such adaptability has always been profit: if there was not still a great deal of money to be made out of movies (as much these days via cable, video and marketing franchises as from movie theatres), there would no longer be a Hollywood. It may be a

3

tourist attraction, but it is definitely not a museum.

The subsidised model for film production is, by contrast, basically a European phenomenon working from a rather different premise, which can perhaps best be described as the 'cultural imperative'. From the mid-1920s, when film first began to be seen as an art form, a number of countries set up systems of subvention and support designed to ensure that national audiences could be supplied with films that spoke the country's language and reflected the country's social and cultural concerns. The prime examples of this kind of film industry are France and Sweden, both of which have established an international reputation for their films and have, more importantly, retained a substantial share of the home market for the home product. Over the past twenty years, West Germany and Italy have developed a variant on this system, adapted to the age of television, in which the film industry's up-start offshoot has its profitability tapped as a way of keeping the cinema as such alive.[1]

Neither Hollywood-style nor state-supported, the British film industry has always fallen more or less disastrously between these two stools. Britain, as economic events have constantly reminded us over the past twenty-five years, is a small country with a sometimes disproportionate belief in her world significance. Whatever this may mean in terms of Britain's world role – and here, recent events have indicated that realities of scale can still occasionally give way to echoes of empire – it has fairly inescapable implications when it comes to film.

The British film industry has traditionally been expected to survive commercially and without any real government aid on a small market that has, moreover, always been loaded against it. The initial problem was competition from Hollywood. The second – and additional – one was competition from television (an industry which *does* receive government support) and, latterly, from home video, in which field Britain has one of the world's highest rates of ownership and rental. There are, of course, less tangible reasons for the historical weakness of the British film industry. First, the arts establishment in Britain has often seemed to have a definite anti-cinematic bias: even when the need for arts subsidies was eventually recognised, film was regarded as somehow less worthy of support than, say, opera or live theatre. Then, there has been the resulting exodus of talented film-makers drawn by the greater creative facilities – and, of course, greater salaries – of Hollywood.

4

But, in the final analysis, it is less a question of attitude than of economics: the British film industry has, since the end of the First World War, staggered from crisis to crisis (with occasional very brief periods of health), because the British market is not large enough to support a film industry built on the classic laissez-faire model, and because government policy has never been sufficiently convinced of either the economic *or* the cultural need for films to do anything which might genuinely rectify the situation. To put it bluntly, we do not seem in any real sense to *need* a film industry in Britain, however much we think we might like one: British cinemas (and, more recently, British television channels and video players) have been kept perfectly well supplied with English-speaking features from across the Atlantic. This rather tends to dull the edge of the 'cultural imperative', since we have never been obliged to watch dubbed films. In producer Leon Clore's memorable phrase, 'if the United States spoke Spanish, we would have a film industry'.[2] And the less easily defined 'need' for British films which reflect British culture and explore matters of concern to British people has never really been recognised at much more than a theoretical level. In any case, this need has been fairly adequately met since the mid-1960s by British television.

All this is not, of course, to say that Britain is a blank page in the history of world cinema. From the pioneering efforts of Cecil Hepworth, through the silent and early sound films of Anthony Asquith, the 1930s British movies of Alfred Hitchcock, the post-war work of David Lean, the late 1950s flowering of talents like Lindsay Anderson, Karel Reisz, Tony Richardson and John Schlesinger, to the more recent movies of a wide spectrum of film-makers from Richard Attenborough, Alan Parker and Ridley Scott, to Peter Greenaway, Bill Forsyth and Bill Douglas, there is – whatever François Truffaut may once arrogantly have asserted – quite clearly something called British cinema.

What is more, there is and, for well over fifty years, always has been a British film industry, at least as far as plant and infrastructure are concerned. Individual studios may have come and gone in the corporate sense, but over the years the production facilities at Elstree, Pinewood and Twickenham have been there to produce films, if and when the funds for film-making have been available. By the same token, the distributors' offices in Wardour Street and the chains of cinemas they have supplied – gradually dwindling over the years and by now prosaically reduced to an unappealing choice

5

between a local Odeon and a local ABC – have maintained a more or less serviceable market outlet for the product.

This industry has, of course, rarely been under totally British control. John Maxwell's British International Pictures (later Associated British Picture Corporation) at Elstree, flour king J. Arthur Rank's bid for the family audience through his Pinewood-based Rank Organisation, and the more recent efforts of Lord Grade's ITC have all, after a more or less long run, failed to survive on the open cinematic market. The smaller, more quality-conscious efforts of Alexander Korda's London Films, and the Gainsborough and Ealing Studios, similarly failed to build lasting operations on early successes, or perhaps failed to adjust to changes in taste and economic climate. In much the same way, the distribution offices in Wardour Street have long been little more than outposts of the Hollywood majors, not radically different in policy and organisation from similar outposts firmly implanted in almost every country in the world.

The changed cinematic climate of the 1980s has certainly given birth to a number of different production and distribution initiatives. But the paradox of an infrastructure without (always) an industry to go with it is one which is central to any understanding of British film. While it may have led to a predominantly mid-Atlantic film culture, it has also accounted more than anything else for the ability of the British film industry to re-emerge, phoenix-like, from its own ashes at regular intervals ever since the advent of the talkies. In addition, it has meant that, while the production facilities at Pinewood and Elstree have recently tended to become overseas bases for proto-Hollywood productions like *Superman* and *Star Wars*, *Yentl*, *Indiana Jones* and *Santa Claus*, they have not degenerated, as did their Spanish equivalents in the 1960s, into mere sources of cheap space and labour. Rather, the British studio complexes have provided work for the cinematographers, art directors, editors, assistant directors, production managers and general technical personnel on whom another aspect of Britain's cinematic reputation has largely rested: that of having the best technicians in the world. Without these, the latest resurgence in British film production could not have taken place. Indeed, the fact that the crews – rather than the directors and the stars – have, over the past decade, maintained the reputation and even the existence of the British film industry, has done much to scotch a myth that has haunted the industry since (at least) World War II: that it is these same crews, as represented by their union, the Association of Cinematograph and Television Technicians, that have held down the British cinema through restrictive manning practices.

The cinema is, and always has been, a pragmatic art form and industry: Bob Dylan's dictum that 'there is no success like failure' could have been made for it. Without going too deep into the realm of metaphysics, it is possible to say that many of the negative developments of the past twenty years have been a necessary cause of the currently hopeful reawakening of the British film industry. The wrong turns of the 1960s and the failures of the 1970s have, in the mid-1980s, produced a situation in which, with adjustments and good will, British films can once more be made.

Other essays in this book will look more closely at particular aspects of the recent revival in British film (and/or the British film industry). But what remains to be done here is to look at two historical developments: the operation of the 'free market' in terms of British cinema, and the various extremely hesitant forms of government intervention in that market. If indeed British cinema has fallen between two stools – condemned to be a commercial operation which can never be commercially viable but which is none the less denied government support – then, in the best diagnostic tradition, the stools need to be analysed.

*A Passage to India*

7

There is not the space here for a history, potted or otherwise, of British film; and besides, enough such histories already exist.[3] What *is* relevant to the present undertaking, however, is an understanding of the historical perspectives which have shaped the British film industry as it exists in the 1980s. In this context, there is one overwhelming truth which has dominated the situation since the mid-1950s and is likely to go on doing so for the foreseeable future: the real crisis in British cinema is not in production but in distribution and exhibition. It is no use British film-makers turning out high-quality films – or films of any quality – if there is no one out there to watch them. And at first – or, for that matter, at second – glance, the realities of cinemagoing in this country are numbing. Over the years, the main indices of cinemagoing in Britain have shown a steady and at times dramatic decline, as the following Figures demonstrate. What must be borne in mind about these Figures is that they reflect the cinemagoing habits of a population of around 55 million people[4] at a time when, elsewhere in the world (and particularly in the United States), the numbers of both cinemas and cinema admissions are beginning to rise after nearly two decades of constant decline.

The three charts are striking, but they are not entirely self-explanatory. Figure 1 (the number of cinemas) indicates two basic stages in the history of British filmgoing. The first is the advent of television, which accounts for the staggering decline in the number of cinemas between 1955 (British television became a two-channel affair in September of that year) and 1970, a period when vast numbers of them were converted into bingo halls and then, with the decline in even *that* form of evening out, into boarded-up eyesores or parking lots. The second is the rationalisation of exhibition outlets through the introduction of multi-screen cinemas in the early 1970s, which briefly halted the decline in overall numbers.

Figure 3 (box office returns) shows the same initial plunge as Figure 1, but begins to level out sooner with the arrival of inflation as a fact of British (and world) economic life in the 1960s. It even begins to rise during the 1970s under the dual impetus of spiralling inflation (between 1960 and 1980, cinema admission prices increased by anything from six to ten times) and the blockbuster films of the second half of the decade, which may have done something to restore the cinemagoing habit, but did little to help the British film industry.

8

Obviously, though, it is Figure 2 which is the most significant: there is no way in which a rise in box office revenue of around 25% between 1950 and 1980 (as seen in Figure 3) can offset the fact that, over the same period, production costs rose by around 20 times. And Figure 2 shows an almost steady decline in admissions, precipitous between 1950 and 1970, levelling off during the 1970s, as though the 100 million barrier was somehow sacred, then finally plunging through that barrier in 1980. What this means, if one

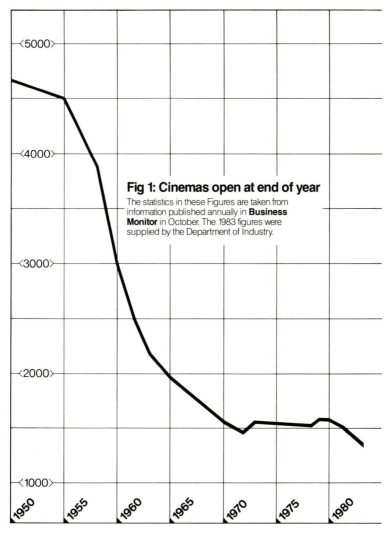

**Fig 1: Cinemas open at end of year**
The statistics in these Figures are taken from information published annually in **Business Monitor** in October. The 1983 figures were supplied by the Department of Industry.

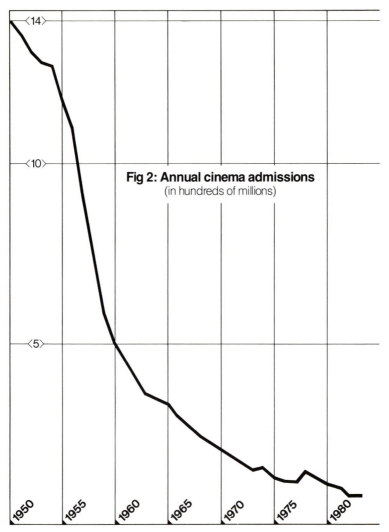

**Fig 2: Annual cinema admissions**
(in hundreds of millions)

〈14〉
〈10〉
〈5〉

1950  1955  1960  1965  1970  1975  1980

divides the population figure into the admissions figure, is that the average Briton goes to the cinema something like once a year, and even less if the population figure is adjusted for those too young to be taken into account. By contrast with the 1945 figure of 1,585 million (or around 30 visits a year), the 1983 cinema admissions figure of 64.35 million, though slightly up on 1982's all-time low, reflects a change in British leisuregoing habits which does little to provide encouragement for a film industry.

But that, unfortunately, is not all. If one scans the list of box-office leaders published annually by *Screen International*, one finds that this decline in overall admission figures is, from the mid-1970s, paralleled by a decline in the number of British films that make it into the list. In 1971, over half the 'top-ten' box-office films in the list were British. Since 1978, that proportion has hovered somewhere between a quarter and a third, and even that figure is inflated by the fact that films like *Superman* are, for

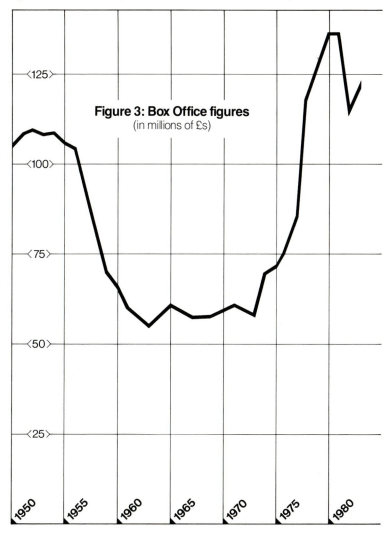

**Figure 3: Box Office figures**
(in millions of £s)

purposes of registration, counted as British. By any criterion, the British film industry is clearly in trouble.

*The Government and the Film Industry*
If government intervention in the film industry has never been especially inspired, it has, in one way or another, been fairly constant. Since the first Cinematograph Act of 1909, there have been twenty-three further pieces of legislation directly related to the cinema.[5] Reading through them is a depressing experience, not merely because the language of enacted legislation is necessarily (and sometimes unnecessarily) turgid, but because, even reading between the lines, it is hard to find anything beyond the most grudging of beliefs that what the French call 'le septième art' deserves support, either from the exchequer or through indirectly supportive legislation. Nor is there any indication that the film *industry* is thought to need any kind of protection, or that any adjustment should be made to a market which is not really 'free'. As Mamoun Hassan, former Managing Director of the National Film Finance Corporation, put it:

> Recently a journalist who had found the Answer[6] suggested that film should be treated no differently from ball-bearings. We should be so lucky. The ball-bearing industry has enjoyed considerable investment from the private sector and has benefited from government intervention.[7]

In film, investment from the private sector has generally been sluggish, and government intervention at best hesitant.

Some of the Acts (1909, 1922, 1952) are concerned only with safety measures to be taken in premises used for film exhibition. The Sunday Entertainments Act of 1932 and the Sunday Cinema Act of 1972 cover, as their names imply, no more than the showing of films on the sabbath. The Cinematograph Films (Animals) Act of 1937 is designed to prevent the showing of films in which unnecessary suffering is caused to animals. And the Cinematograph (Amendment) Act of 1982 is a specific piece of legislation designed to eliminate hard-core porn cinemas, interesting in that it is the only one of the twenty-four to touch on the question of censorship. This is an area of activity which, since the setting-up of the non-statutory British Board of Film Censors in 1912, has been left to self-regulation on the part of the industry itself, with all the advantages and drawbacks that entails.

This leaves a ˏdozen or so pieces of legislation which are concerned with regulating and, occasionally, protecting the British film industry. They do so in two basic ways: by attempting to limit the number of foreign (mainly American) films; and by channelling a small percentage of the box-office take back into film production. The first important piece of legislation in this respect in the Cinematograph Films Act of 1927 which, in addition to protecting exhibitors against the notorious blind-booking clauses favoured by the American majors (whereby, in order to get the key films from a company's annual production slate, the exhibitor was obliged to take on a number of other films sight unseen), made the first of many attempts to require renters and exhibitors to handle British-made films and so stem the Hollywood flood. It did so by means of a quota of British films, starting at $7\frac{1}{2}\%$ for renters and 5% for exhibitors in 1929, and supposedly rising to 20% for both by 1938. Its provisions were necessarily complicated, involving compulsory registration of films and methods of calculation which multiplied the footage of the film by the number of screenings. But perhaps its most interesting section was the one which, for the first time, attempted to define what was meant by a 'British film' – a definition which has exercised critics and historians ever since. Under the 1927 Act, a film was British if it was made by a British subject or a British company, its studio scenes were photographed in a studio in the British Empire, the writer was British, and not less than 75% of the salaries, wages and payments for labour and services (with certain exemptions allowing the use of one foreign star) were paid to British subjects.

In time, this Act led to the emergence of the 'quota quickie', a cheaply made film which enabled the quota to be met but was clearly contrary to the spirit of the Act. Paradoxically, the quota quickie may have done more to harm the British film industry than the Act did to protect it, since it established a connection in the minds of cinemagoers between a British film and a shoddy one, thereby consolidating the belief that all the best films came from Hollywood. At the same time, however, it did encourage the various American majors to set up operations in Britain; and this, while it extended the colonisation of British film culture by Hollywood, also provided a certain crucial amount of encouragement in the field of skills and facilities.

The Cinematograph Films Act of 1938 attempted to rectify the quota quickie situation by allowing a British film to be counted as

13

double or even treble for quota purposes, provided it had cost more than a certain amount: a film costing between £22,500 and £37,500, or £3–5 per foot, counted double; one costing over £37,500 counted treble. The 1938 Act also extended the quotas for a further ten years, recognising a shortfall in the 1938 figures set by the previous Act, and hoping for a quota of 30% for renters and 25% for exhibitors by 1948. It also took a first positive step towards encouraging the industry beyond quota arrangements by setting up the Cinematograph Films Council 'to keep under review the progress of the cinematograph industry in Great Britain', and to report annually to and advise the Board of Trade on 'any matter relating to the cinematograph film industry in which the advice of the Council is sought by the Board' – a form of wording which left the CFC little room to take the initiative. The Cinematograph Films Act of 1948 introduced further modifications to the arrangements and somewhat extended the advisory powers of the CFC; and the Cinematograph Films Act of 1960 consolidated previous quota legislation and set a date of 1967 for an end to the quota system. In fact, the system was extended beyond 1967, and did not finally come to an end until 1982, when it was abolished by Statutory Instrument.

By this time, however, the focus of government legislation had moved away from what was, in effect, a form of import control (which had caused a major crisis between Britain and Hollywood in 1948), and in the direction of providing more active support for film production in Britain. The key Act here was the Cinematograph Film Production (Special Loans) Act of 1949, which set up the National Film Finance Corporation. This was to be the only direct form of government involvement in the field of commercial film production in Britain. With an initial credit limit of £5 million, the NFFC was

> to make, during the five years beginning with the passing of this Act, loans to be employed in financing the production or distribution of cinematograph films to persons who, in the judgement of the Corporation, while having reasonable expectations of being able to arrange for the production and distribution of cinematograph films on a commercially successful basis, are not for the time being in a position to obtain adequate financial facilities for the purpose on reasonable terms from an appropriate source.

In other words, film-makers with viable projects who couldn't raise the money could turn to the NFFC.

Initially, this worked well enough since, in the early years, the NFFC was basically called upon to 'top up' the budgets of British films made by more or less established studios, providing no more than 30% of the budget, much like any industrial credit organisation. In effect, the NFFC was a film bank. Over the years, however, the studio system in Britain collapsed, and the NFFC was called upon to fund less films but to provide a much larger slice of their budgets (while remaining, however, more a midwife than a parent).

Under these circumstances, the requirement that the NFFC should fund only films with a 'reasonable' chance of commercial success became something of a problem. While it may have suited a regular production situation, it was much less straightforwardly applicable to one in which each film had to be planned and budgeted separately in a highly volatile market. After all, if a film had a reasonable chance of commercial success on that market, it was arguable that it should not really need funding from a non-commercial source, least of all in the eyes of a government which believes that, if it sinks, that's because nature put holes in it. In the current context, the ability to set up an advance distribution deal for a film is the only real indication of commercial feasibility. And that distribution deal should provide a fair proportion of the production money, and make the rest of it comparatively easy to raise. If there is no proper distribution deal, the chances of commercial success are probably less than 'reasonable'. To a certain extent, then, there is, in 1980s terms, a contradiction built into the NFFC's charter. Nevertheless, this has not stopped it being a vital force in British film production since its inception, costing the Treasury a mere £11 million over a thirty-year period, and helping to fund some 360 films in the process.

The original 1949 Act gave the NFFC a scant five years. This was modified by an identically named Act in 1952, which empowered the NFFC to borrow up to a further £2 million from sources other than the Board of Trade, and another Act in 1954 which extended the loan period from five to eight years, and made special provisions for loans which could not be repaid – the first (tacit) recognition of the need for a government subsidy to the British film industry, though in the characteristically negative and hand-to-mouth form of allowing debts to be written off rather than offering up-front money.

The final – and initially most promising – form of government intervention came in the Cinematograph Films Act of 1957. That Act, in addition to extending the functions of the NFFC for a further period (done again in 1970 and again in 1980, another instance of the government's hand-to-mouth approach), made law what had previously been a voluntary levy on exhibition (known as Eady money), under which a proportion of the box office receipts was channelled back into the production of British films. Under the 1957 Act, a twelfth of the price of every cinema ticket was to be

---

**British film production levels rely mainly on American finance and on its ability to service national and international television and cable operations. No reliance can be put on this boom period continuing for more than a year or so – if the dollar/pound exchange rate deteriorates, as far as America is concerned, so will our film production level. Particularly with the Government's negation of their responsibility as outlined in the Film Policy White Paper.**

**It seems absolutely incredible that on one hand the White Paper compliments and congratulates all concerned in the magnificent technological and artistic achievements of our film production, and then incredibly states that by axing all that has supported this high level of production such as tax relief, the National Film Finance Corporation, Eady Levy, Cinema Exhibition quota, and Levy on film video tape, it still expects a British Film Production Industry to maintain its present buoyant level.**

**Alan Sapper, General Secretary ACTT**

---

paid back into a British Film Fund, and this was to be used to finance the NFFC, to provide grants for the National Film School, the BFI Production Board and the Children's Film Foundation.[8] The remainder of the money was then to be distributed to the producers of British films as defined by a set of regulations drawn up by the Board of Trade which are not substantially different from those laid out in the 1927 Act.

The principle was simple, but the arithmetic was complicated. The actual sum redistributed to producers was to be determined by the relationship between the amount of money left in the Fund after various fixed payments had been made, and the total amount taken at the box office by films registered as British. Thus, if British films took £4 million and the Fund stood at £1 million, the pay-out rate that year would be 25% (i.e. an individual producer would receive 25% of his or her film's box office returns in Eady money). In effect, this tended to mean two things: that the most successful films got the most Eady money (and conversely, those which needed it most got least); and that there was a strong incentive for loopholes to be found whereby a film could be registered as British without it being so in much more than a legal sense. In general, though, Eady worked well enough in the early years, providing a useful way of channelling money back into production. That it gradually became less useful has to do with circumstances that perhaps should have been, but were not, foreseen.

If the 1960s was the decade of TV, the 1980s has been the decade of video. In both these media (which, in terms of how the viewer views the image, are the same), film has been a crucial element, overwhelmingly so in the case of video. Though figures are hard to come by, it is a fair bet that more people are now watching films than ever before in Britain. But they are not watching them in cinemas. Eady money has, therefore, dwindled from a stream to a trickle. Paradoxically, it has, at the same time, become a heavier burden on the already depressed exhibition business. Thus, while the Cinematograph Exhibitors' Association has been lobbying

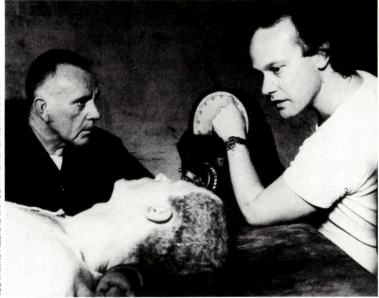

*1984*: Mike Radford with John Hurt and Richard Burton

(successfully) for the abolition of Eady, producers, led by David Puttnam and the Association of Independent Producers, have been campaigning for it to be supplemented or replaced by a levy on blank video tapes and some kind of levy on films shown on television.[9]

All this has taken place in the context of the Thatcher government's enormously protracted, multi-Minister review of film legislation, which culminated in a White Paper on *Film Policy* published in July 1984, and a new Films Act which applies the principles of the 'free market' with a vengeance. This Act abolishes Eady, but replaces it with nothing; privatises the NFFC (under the joint aegis of Rank, Thorn-EMI and Channel 4); and generally creates a vacuum in government film policy the like of which has not existed since before the original Cinematograph Films Act of 1927. All this, it is ironical to note, on the eve of the government-sponsored British Film Year, a promotional jamboree designed to celebrate the British film 'renaissance'.

Such, then, is the background to the British film industry and to British cinema in general in the 1980s: a vanishing audience, a struggling industry and an indifferent, if not hostile, state. That there is a British film industry at all in 1985 is something of a matter for wonder. That it should be going through a 'renaissance' looks little short of a miracle.

# 2

# New audiences, new films

Continuing his introductory survey, **Nick Roddick**
looks at the current state of film production and the way
it is adapting to the needs of a shrinking but more
varied cinema audience and a television industry whose
audiences show an undiminishing appetite for films.

In the first half of the 1980s, a number of things have altered in the world of British film, making the prospects in some ways brighter than they have been at any time since the late 1950s. Then, a literary revival was paralleled by the emergence of a generation of film-makers, not so much from within the industry itself as from the theatre and the still small-scale British Film Institute. In the late 1950s, the country was on the verge of an economic boom which would soon be summed up in Harold Macmillan's catchphrase, 'You've never had it so good'. But the same could not really be said of the film industry; and the cinematic renaissance of the 1950s foundered for want of adequate finance, sufficient commitment on the part of the production companies, and production structures which could really take advantage of the flowering of talents.

In the 1980s, nobody would seriously suggest that we've never had it so good. But there is the same intangible promise of an interest in 'British' subjects, represented by films like *The Long Good Friday*, *Chariots of Fire*, Bill Forsyth's features *Gregory's Girl*,

*Local Hero* and *Comfort and Joy*, Michael Radford's *Another Time, Another Place* and *1984*, and the parallel 'Irish renaissance' of Neil Jordan's *Angel* and *The Company of Wolves*, and Pat O'Connor's *Cal* (the last two entirely British in terms of finance). It is, however, in more tangible areas that the prospect of a continued revival in British film really lies – in the existence of more realistic structures of production and possibilities of finance. The question, after all, is not whether there *ought* to be British films, but whether there *can* be.

A couple of preliminary observations need to be made, however. The first is that, while the previous chapter was concerned with economics and legislation, artistic questions are also clearly relevant to any discussion of British cinema now. And, in this respect, the late 1970s and early 1980s have seen the emergence of a wide range of highly talented film-makers from a variety of sources, few of which were those of the traditional film industry. Some of them, like Alan Parker, Ridley Scott and Hugh Hudson, came from the world of advertising, bringing to feature films a great deal of technical skill and, more importantly, the ability to conceive of films in terms of their visual impact. While this may at times have led to a style of film-making which goes for the immediate effect at the expense of a more graduated approach – a charge which can be levelled against Ridley Scott's *Alien* and *Blade Runner*, and to an even greater extent against his brother Tony Scott's *The Hunger* (largely shot in Britain, but set in New York) – it has emphatically rescued British cinema from the pedestrian blandness which often seemed to be its only attribute in the immediate post-war years.

Others among the new generation of film-makers[1] have come from television docudrama, like Roland Joffe, whose debut feature was the $11 million *The Killing Fields*, or else have come *back* from television, like Stephen Frears, who with *The Hit* in 1984 made his first feature for over a decade. Others, in contrast, came from the very limited subsidised sector. Peter Greenaway, whose *The Draughtman's Contract* had a critical and even a commercial success beyond all expectation for so experimental a film, spent a number of years working on documentaries for the government's Central Office of Information, in addition to making his own films with minimal financial support from various arts-funding bodies. Ed Bennett, whose feature *Ascendancy* shared the Golden Bear at the 1983 Berlin Film Festival, made his first films for the Arts Council and the Regional Arts Associations. Mike Radford, whose

20

*Another Time, Another Place* was very warmly received at the Directors' Fortnight at Cannes in 1983, and whose film of George Orwell's *1984* has been an enormous success in Britian, Europe and Australia, is a Film School graduate who also worked for the COI and in television before making his first theatrical feature. Richard Eyre, whose first feature, *The Ploughman's Lunch*, was both critically and commercially successful, came from the theatre. Chris Petit, director of *Radio On, An Unsuitable Job for a Woman, Flight to Berlin* and *Chinese Boxes*, was – and still is – a critic. BFI funding has been crucial in encouraging films like Sally Potter's *The Gold Diggers*, with its all-woman crew, and films which deal with Britain's ethnic community, like Menelik Shabazz's *Burning an Illusion*, and *Rough Cut and Ready Dubbed* (directed by Hasan Shah and Don Shaw). All are films which could not or would not have been made ten years ago, and the variety of routes which led to their making is symptomatic of the diversity of the current British films scene.

Equally important in this respect is an apparent readiness on the part of audiences to show an interest in British film subjects, although the problems of distribution are such that the smaller and more 'difficult' films have not been widely seen outside (and

21

occasionally inside) London. This is indicative of a wider problem: that it is virtually impossible for any kind of British film to recoup its costs on the home theatrical market. This has a number of implications for the British film industry. Firstly, full-scale commercial films like *The French Lieutenant's Woman*, *Local Hero* or *The Killing Fields* must of necessity have an overseas (basically, an American) distribution deal set up before they can go in front of the cameras (though Virgin were prepared to risk going without one in order to get *1984* released in the year in which it was 'set').

Secondly, although the cinema audience may have shrunk, the same is by no means true of the audience for moving images as a whole, and any examination of British film in the 1980s must

---

**There's nothing coherent about British film (why should there be?), so what to say? Theatrical, literary, documentary, hand to mouth, a consensus of good taste, a deadly respectableness. A lack of myth. Too little, too late. Directing a film in Britain: like middle-management in a car plant. Excessive overheads, working lunches. A question of attitudes and not much more. There are exceptions but not enough. A renaissance? (Please, let's forget this word.) A brief revival in production perhaps, but is it cinema?**

**Christopher Petit, Director**

---

recognise that the traditional frontier between film and television is no longer a realistic one. Thirdly, while the somewhat ambiguous but none the less bright aspirations of the 1960s have long since faded, the efforts at setting up an alternative distribution circuit made at the time by organisations like The Other Cinema have ultimately borne fruit in a network of small film outlets, mainly in London, but also in the provinces (where they are, of course, supplemented by the BFI's regional film theatres).

There is, then, an audience available for both kinds of British film – the large-scale commercial and the small-scale experimental and/or radical. But tapping that audience is still difficult. And it does remain true that, despite a number of hopeful developments over the last couple of years (for example, the BFI-initiated plan to get local chain cinemas to show less obviously commercial films one day a week), the structures of distribution and exhibition in Britain offer nowhere near the same signs of promise as does the production industry, nor do they seem likely to benefit in the foreseeable future from the kind of inspired experiment currently under way in France.[2]

Beyond the question of distribution and exhibition (dealt with by Archie Tait later in the book), a full picture of the state of British film in the 1980s necessarily consists of three segments: the commercial sector; the subsidised sector; and the relationship between film and television. Obviously, there is a degree of overlap between these areas – the commercial sector makes little distinction between film and television; television is itself in part (in very large part) a subsidised art form – but the division remains useful for the purposes of this discussion.

### The Commercial Sector

For nearly fifty years, the main source of commercial film production in Britain was the studio system, a scaled-down version of Hollywood. By the end of the 1970s, however, this form of film production had all but collapsed. A small number of films put together more or less in the old manner are still made in Britain – the Joan Collins vehicle, *Nutcracker*, for instance; the TV spin-off *The Boys in Blue*, or action movies like *Who Dares Wins* and the two *Wild Geese* films. Moreover, Thorn-EMI, direct descendant of the ABPC Elstree operation, currently has an interesting slate of films in preparation, and Rank shows signs of becoming active once more. But the main focus of interest has undoubtedly shifted elsewhere. The nearest thing to a pattern for commercial filmmaking in Britain is now represented by films which are funded on an individual basis, with packages put together around a particular property – a subject, a director, a star – whose commercial potential is assessed on a one-off basis. *The French Lieutenant's Woman*, for example, was put together by producer Leon Clore in that way, while the Sean Connery Bond comeback, *Never Say Never Again*, was the result of a financial deal of *Citizen Kane*-like complexity. The main – indeed, almost the only – way this can be done is by means of a pre-sale to an American distributor, who then puts up a certain amount of the money and, more importantly, makes it possible for the rest of the money to be raised. Films *can* be made without a pre-sale, but since this represents the litmus paper of commercial success, it is difficult to do so.

Even so, a substantial proportion of the funds still needs to be raised on the open money market. Although the relationship between the film industry and the City of London has degenerated

23

badly over the past fifteen or twenty years, there are now signs that the City in general, and the major pension funds and merchant banks in particular, are once again ready to put money into feature films: the kudos gained by *Chariots of Fire* and *Gandhi* is, perhaps, not entirely intangible.[3] In the early 1980s, the raising of money for film production was, additionally, given a boost by a certain number of tax incentives introduced by the Conservative government as a way of helping industrial production in general. Foremost among these was the tax write-off scheme, which enabled financial houses to write off 100% of film production costs in the first year. This scheme, discussed in Chapter 3, is now being phased out, however, and opinions vary as to the effect this will have on finance for film-making. Nevertheless, money has been forthcoming and films have been made. Some of the companies who have worked in this context are discussed by Robert Murphy in Chapter 4.

As far as directors are concerned, there are, within the commercial sector, a number of undeniably 'British' film-makers like Alan Parker, Ridley Scott, Peter Yates and Tony Richardson whose work has recently been more often than not in the United States, but whose films are still the work of British film-makers. Hemingway, after all, remained an 'American' writer while working in Paris, Spain or Cuba, and Britain's emigré film-makers (many of whom in fact continue to live and often work in Britain) are as much a part of the current British film scene as is the more obviously indigenous product.

### The Subsidised Sector

By definition, the films produced in the subsidised sector in Britain are made on much smaller budgets and represent a rather different kind of film-making – more risky, more experimental and, of course, more 'difficult', both artistically and as a proposition for wider distribution. Over the past three or four years, however, films which have been partly or wholly funded from this sector have opened up a kind of film-making in this country which one would have despaired of seeing ten years ago, resulting in films which deal with specific areas of national experience – a kind of cinema which was familiar enough in Europe, but which has not happened on this side of the Channel, because of the falling-between-two-stools syndrome discussed in the previous chapter.

Subsidised film-making in Britain comes under three main headings: the now to be dismantled National Film Finance Corporation, British Film Institute, and Regional Arts Associations and workshops. The NFFC is (or was, in its 'public' incarnation) obliged to operate quasi-commercially, though the shift in the production situation and the size of the funds made available to it (around £1.5 million) necessarily restricts the kind of films it can invest in and the size of the investment it can make. As Mamoun Hassan, the NFFC's former managing director put it, 'resources dictate policy'.

One of its most notable successes of the 1980s has been Jerzy Skolimowski's *Moonlighting*, a film whose history aptly indicates just why the NFFC was so vital to British film production. The idea – about a group of Poles who are in London at the time of the Polish crisis, and thus obviously very time-specific – was brought to the Corporation's script development subsidiary, the National Film Development Fund, shortly before Christmas 1981. Money was made available for development, and the script was completed early in the New Year. By February, the film was in production, and was completed in time to be shown at Cannes in May 1982. As with nearly all its projects, the NFFC was not sole financier for *Moonlighting* (other funds came from theatre and film impresario Michael White, and from Channel 4); but, without the NFFC, it

Jeremy Irons in *Moonlighting*

25

seems unlikely that the film would have been made at all, let alone made in so short a time. The NFFC was a vital part of British film culture through the dark period of the late 1970s, and its seems absurd that it should, in effect, be wound up at a time when it could play an even more useful role in the revival in British film production. But such are the dictates of free market policies.

The BFI Production Board, whose origins date back to Michael Balcon's Experimental Film Fund of the early 1950s, has only really come to play a major role in British film production over the past two or three years, with a string of films – *Ascendancy*, *The Draughtsman's Contract*, *The Gold Diggers*, *Flight to Berlin*, and the Terence Davies trilogy – which have been well received at film festivals, and have had limited distribution both at home and abroad. It does not have the NFFC's 'commercial' imperative: its role lies in the encouragement of experiment and innovation, and in providing film-makers with the opportunity to make the sort of films which, at first sight, do not meet the NFFC's criteria. The Production Board's film-making budget reached a peak in 1981/82, when over £1 million was available for production (including co-production). It has since declined, mainly as a result of the BFI's need to siphon funds into regional production. Artistically, the Board has broken new ground and nurtured new talents in a way which is bound, if only indirectly, to feed back into the commercial system, sponsoring the kind of stylistic advances without which any film culture will soon die. But it, too, is unlikely to survive the government's latest Films Act, since Eady was a major source of its funding.

The final area of subsidised production is one which is especially essential in an age in which the culture is predominantly audio-visual: the production of small-scale, local projects, designed to give members of a particular community hands-on experience of film and video, and to enable specific local problems to be examined in either documentary or fictional form. Here, for once, distribution is not a major issue: the process is more important than the product. The focus in this case has been the Regional Arts Associations and the various film and video Workshops which have been established throughout the country with government, BFI and local authority funding. In this sector, the budgets are smaller still – a 16mm film or video project costing £10,000 or under is not unusual – and the degree of interaction with the film industry or with any form of commercial film production is strictly limited. But the Workshops in particular play an important part in British film culture, and one which has been recognised by the ACTT's Workshops Declaration, which allows for film-making of this kind to take place outside the terms of the Union's normal requirements on remuneration and manning so long as the workshops operate non-commercially.

*Film and Television*
Since the late 1940s, when it first began to have a real impact on Hollywood, television has been a crucial influence on the film industry. Initially, this influence was entirely negative: TV took audiences away from the cinemas and, to compound the insult, bought up the studios' film libraries and began screening them. With the advent of cable operations like Home Box Office in the United States at the beginning of this decade, the as yet unfulfilled promise of similar operations in Europe by the mid-1980s, and the headlong growth in home video ownership and rental, the television set's onslaught on the film industry has begun to look like a rout.

But this is only true if one persists in seeing the relationship between film and television in terms of the abrasive rivalries of the 1950s. In the present context, and above all in Britain, the relationship between the two arms of the moving image industry is more symbiotic than it has ever been. There are a number of reasons for this. Firstly, it is no longer possible for anyone professionally involved in the film industry – as performer, producer, director, writer or technician – to make a living without occasional recourse to television, whether in TV advertising or in programme production. Secondly – and relatedly – in a culture dominated by television, the small screen provides much of the training in all fields that was once supplied by the B-movie arm of the film industry and, even now, is only partly supplied by the National Film School and other educational institutions. And thirdly, all of the major production companies and the vast majority of the smaller ones are as much involved in supplying product for – or selling it to – television as they are in making films for theatrical release. With the decline in cinemas and cinemagoing, the selling of films to television is a vital part of the marketing strategy of any film production company.

It is, unfortunately, more in the interests of the film industry to recognise the nature of this relationship than it is in the interest of television. In one sense, film and television stand in the same relationship to one another now as did theatre and film in the early days of the cinema: the one has usurped the other. But there is one crucial difference: film provides much of television's product. And it is this recognition by Britain's newest television station, Channel 4, which has seemed to offer some of the brightest possibilities for film production in Britain in the 1980s.

By the time it first went on the air in early November 1982, Channel 4 had commissioned or part-funded a whole string of 'feature films' for its 'Film on Four' slot, some of which, like *The Ploughman's Lunch*, *Another Time*, *Another Place* and *Angel*, are at the heart of the 'renaissance'. Part of the deal had been that the films would be allowed a theatrical release – or 'window' – before their television screening (a variant on the German model). Initially, this seemed to be in the interest of both the film-makers and Channel 4: the former would have a chance to show their films in the place for which they were primarily intended, with better picture definition and a more sustained audience attention, while the interest and (hopefully) good reviews generated by the theatrical release would make the film something of an event when it was screened on television. In practice, though, the system has

*Angel*

28

not worked out quite as well as expected, since audiences have proved reluctant to turn out for films they knew they could soon see on television (and distributors, as a result, reluctant to handle them), while Channel 4 has understandably wanted to see its investments on the screen as soon as possible ('We are not,' as one Channel 4 executive put it, 'in the archive business'). The honeymoon period between Channel 4 and the independent film-makers is now over, but Channel 4 remains an extremely promising (not to say vital) source of production finance for British film, not least because the money it puts up (up to £650,000 for certain projects) is not an advance, but a tangible sum of up-front money which can act as the bedrock of the budget.

In broader terms, however, the change in the market for moving images – from cinema towards television and video – has other implications for the future of film in Britain which must, at some stage, be recognised if the film industry is to survive. The first implication is crucial and, in the present context, crushingly negative: it is, in the final analysis, television which determines that the British film industry is not operating on a free market. The BBC gets its money from a licence fee controlled by the government, and the independent ITV companies are effectively subsidised by being granted franchises for particular geographical areas in which they will hold a monopoly on television advertising. Television is, therefore, as both the NFFC and the AIP have been eager to point out, a duopoly whose privileged position in the moving image market is built into its various charters. If it was simply in competition with film on an open market, the implications of this situation would be harder to argue. But it is not. Television is protected by the government, while the film industry is expected to sail unaided on the seas of monetarism.

More insidiously, television is a buyer of the film industry's products, and relies quite heavily on those products – as a glance at the trailers for Christmas programmes will indicate – for audience-building. Yet British television pays some of the lowest rates in the world for the films it shows. This is, of course, a direct result of the duopoly situation, and may just be modified by the advent of cable television on a large scale in Britain. As things now stand, however, television is able effectively to dictate the purchase price for all but the most massive of holiday blockbusters (where one channel is genuinely in competition with the other): after all, buying in a film is a lot cheaper than making a programme. To see how this operates, one has only to compare the situation of films sold to television, with the televising of football: in the latter area, the potential emergence in 1983 of a private cable interest as a competitor to the two major networks caused the asking price to rocket. That is a 'free market situation'. The one in which the film industry is expected to operate is not.

This shift towards television and video as a major market for recent films is a fact of the past decade. Before that, the notion that television showed only old movies remained essentially correct. But now, as the holdbacks get shorter and shorter, especially for Film on Four, television is a direct competitor with the cinema, but with the odds stacked heavily in its favour. Any fiscal support for film ought to recognise this. Recent proposals by the AIP called for a levy on films shown on television ($\frac{1}{4}$p per viewer per film) and on the sale of blank video cassettes (£1 per cassette), with the proceeds paid into an 'Industry Subscription Fund'. This would, claimed the AIP, channel an initial £35 million a year back into the production of films. It is a proposal which has received widespread support from the industry, but has obviously been less warmly greeted by the television companies and the cassette retailers. Nevertheless, something along these lines is necessary if British film, 'commercial' or 'subsidised', is to survive: the British film industry of the 1980s exists within a world where the dividing line between its two major outlets – the cinema and television – has all but disappeared (except, of course, in the eyes of the government). What is more, the two industries are interdependent to such an extent that support for film production can, in the long run, only help television in terms of both quality and profitability. 'British film now' is a more accurate term than 'British cinema now'.

# 3

# Finding the money

Money and art have always had an uneasy coexistence.
But film is a business as much as it is an art.
And, argues **Matthew Silverstone**, as he looks at the
current state of film financing in Britain, it is time the country's
film-makers came to terms with that reality.

Traditionally, British film finance has been obtained from a relatively small number of sources, chiefly from major distributors like Rank and EMI, and selected merchant banks. An idea would be conceived and a script written; the producer would then peddle the idea from finance source to finance source, in the hope that one of them would be interested in backing the project. If this proved unsuccessful, the producer could, as a last resort, attempt to raise the finance from an individual backer who might be attracted to the project. The likelihood of finding such a backer was, however, remote.

The most attractive method of financing a film from a producer's point of view was via the 100% involvement of a major distributor. A project that required, say, a $10 million budget would be financed solely by this distributor, in return for certain guaranteed distribution rights on the British and/or US market. What made this especially attractive was that it relieved the producer of trying to raise money from many different sources, all of whom were likely to negotiate different terms and want a different return on their investment. It also meant that the sale of rights in other markets would bring in a direct profit. What made this situation rare, of course, was that the distributor was unlikely to hand the producer profits on a plate.

Generally speaking, though, a film had to have a theatrical (i.e. cinema) distributor, or it would not be viable. If the film was not accepted in advance by a large distribution house, it was virtually impossible to raise money from alternative sources.

In recent years, however, there has been a huge growth in the so-called 'ancillary markets', such as television, video and cable; and this change has also made itself felt in the area of financing. Video companies such as Embassy may now purchase the world-wide video rights in advance for a sum in the region of 20% of the total budget. Because of the increased competition among video distributors for software, companies have been forced into the position where they have to participate at an earlier stage of a film's development. Indeed, not only are they beginning to be involved in pre-sales, but they are becoming co-producers as well. Entertainment in Video, a fast-growing video company, has participated in ten films as co-producer, providing risk capital in return for an equity stake in the film. Other video companies, such as Atlantis Video, are now going the whole hog and acting as producers: they provide the seed money for a film's development, organise the budget, cast the film and arrange pre-sale deals, just like a production house. In return, they keep a large equity stake in the film, together with the United Kingdom video rights.

Cable is also becoming an increasing source of film finance, though mainly in the US. The US cable company, Home Box Office, is rapidly becoming the world's largest financier of films. But such developments have as yet to make any real impact on British production finance. Although a number of British producers have been able to do deals with US cable consortia, what the latter are really looking for is software that will appeal directly to the American market – something that British producers have not generally been capable of providing in the past.

Record companies such as Virgin, A & M and Charisma have also been a source of finance in 1980s. Virgin, in particular, has committed £60 million plus to film production, though this may be affected by changing tax legislation and the success of their first slate of films.

Even with a wider range of potential investors, however, some degree of pre-sale is generally essential for a producer. And, despite the increasing number of alternative sources of finance, the more traditional sources of money – the institutional investors – remain crucial to the success of the British film industry. These have, in the past, shown a strong reluctance to have anything to do with that industry – something for which they are generally held in low regard by the industry itself. A lot of rhetoric has been expended on the City's attitude to Wardour Street. The City's wariness, however, has both historical precedent and financial commonsense to back it

---

**British films have made a fresh breakthrough into the international market. This is wonderful, but it carries dangers with it. It means close involvement with the American industry and the risk of being swamped by Hollywood. Somehow we have to learn to compete with American professionalism at the creative level without losing our freshness and reality – the things they lack. It begins with scripts. Our writers must be fostered, must be disciplined, and must be protected from the transatlantic gales. It was mainly thanks to our writers that British television drama became the envy of the world, and now television is failing them. If our film industry makes the same mistake, we shall lose our toehold on the future.**

**James Brabazon, Producer**

---

up. And, in a book on contemporary British cinema, the reasons for that attitude seem worth investigating.

Experience is a quality that all investors look for. If a producer requires an investment of $2 million, those individuals or companies assessing the potential returns and risk variables will want to be assured that their money will be handled professionally. One means of assessing such a variable is to look at the producer's previous experience. A producer who has proved in the past that he can bring a film in within the specified budget will, at the simplest level, appeal more to a financier than one who keeps asking for more money because he has been unable to control the budget or handle the demands of a particular director.

Experience, however, is not a prerequisite for *raising* finance. Because of the nature of the job, the producer can raise finance by selling the experience of the rest of the team (in this instance, I am using the word 'producer' to describe the executive/associate producer, whose job it is to raise the capital for the film). If the producer can show that he has employed professionals to analyse the film's potential markets, negotiate a percentage of the pre-sold distribution for it, and recruited people with a proven track record to make it, it is not necessary for the executive producer to have actual production experience.

The 'line' producer – the person who spends the money on actually making the film – does, however, need experience, for it makes little financial sense to allocate, say, $8 million to an individual who has had no training in how to spend the money efficiently.

The packages that interest film financiers are the same as those that interest distributors: both are looking at the commercial viability of the project. Financiers are understandably not interested in financing a film that looks unlikely to show a profit – unless, of course, there is some tax advantage to be had from doing so. Different qualities are needed in a film package, depending upon the different qualities that the film itself must have. An ideal package would be one where a producer had succeeded in securing 100% of the budget in pre-sold distribution guarantees. Under such an arrangement, the producer would have negotiated with

Burt Lancaster in *Local Hero*

various organisations, such as theatrical distributors and buyers for ancillary markets, to guarantee him a sum that would eventually add up to the cost of the picture. In this way, no risk is borne by the financier, because his money is guaranteed in pre-sales.

But even so, this does not guarantee that money can be raised from financiers, because of the credit rating that banks put on distributors. Even though the money appears to be guaranteed, the bank may not consider the distributor credit-worthy. It is, therefore, very important to have financial evidence about the distributor's financial position: some banks even demand an up-to-date balance sheet.

Such situations arise infrequently for the independent producer, however. Achieving pre-sold distribution guarantees for a producer offering a film that is not aimed at a 'majority' audience is extremely difficult: majority audience films are precisely what attract financiers. Nevertheless, some degree of pre-sold distribution is essential when soliciting money from financial institutions. ICFC will, for example, finance films only when the producer has pre-sales to offer; Rediffusion insists that the producer obtain 25% of the budget in pre-sold distribution before it will consider a proposition.

A second factor that used to be considered important was having 'star' names in the film package, whether they were the names of actors, directors or even the producer. This has changed. At the present time, 'names' are important but not vital, especially when the producer is concerned with making a small-budget feature where the cost of hiring stars is prohibitive. However, if it follows that the distributor wants names before guaranteeing any pre-sale, then it follows that the financier, who is equally concerned with securing pre-sales, will also want them. Columbia Pictures, a major distributor, uses a loose criterion that, when a film costs more than $5 million, a producer must offer a star, preferably a star director. Columbia believes that a star director with a proven track-record of profit-making films will be more likely to repeat this success. When one is gambling with large sums of money, this principle becomes very important.

A recent arrival on the film-making scene but by now a vital consideration to a financial institution is a completion guarantee. One of the major problems that face a producer is the possibility that the film will run over budget. If this happens, whether through bad management or bad luck, the producer is going to have to approach the backers for more money. To forestall such a situation, financiers ask the producer to secure a completion guarantee. This is, in effect, an insurance policy taken out on the film by the producer. It means that, if the film runs over budget, the financier will not be required to pay any extra, because this will come from the company that negotiates the completion guarantee.

It is common knowledge that investors like to spread their risk, and the film business is no exception. The film industry is classified as a high-risk investment, and few investment companies like to get involved because it is not traditionally part of their portfolio. Similarly, investment companies analyse the risk in relation to its potential return: high-risk investments imply a potentially high rate of return. Until recently, the British film industry was seen as simply not worth investing in, because the likely rewards did not justify the risk. It took the success of *Chariots of Fire* and *Gandhi* to cause investment houses to reappraise the film industry as a possibility for profitable investment.

One of the ways of spreading the risk in the film business is by investing on a portfolio basis. If the risk can be spread in what is, by definition, a high-risk business, then so much the better. It is for this reason that an offer of a portfolio of films looks more attractive to a high-risk investor than a one-off investment in a single feature film. In the jargon of finance, this is referred to as cross-collateralisation – that is, offsetting losses against profits to balance out to a profitable outcome.

If a producer offers seven films to a financier, the statistical likelihood is that four will make a loss, two will just about break even, and one will make enough money to offset the losses and turn the portfolio overall into a profitable investment. It is this type of investment that most financiers look for. Unfortunately, though, there are at the moment few film companies which can offer such a portfolio.

Finally, all financiers prefer to invest in a group of individuals, rather than in just one. In other words, it is not the individual that interests the financiers, but a team. A team whose members have a proven ability to manage money, rather than specifically films, is the sort that appeals to investors. This is not a new phenomenon, but one on which investors have based many of their decisions. It is reckoned that a management team is more likely than an individual to treat money with financial respect and professionalism. Also, a team comprising lawyers, accountants and businessmen can provide legal and professional services that might not be readily available to an individual producer.

The chance of a producer or even a production team raising money from an institutional investor is, however, also dependent on external factors, such as the prevailing tax laws. Merchant banks first became interested in financing feature films in Britain five years ago, as a result of Inland Revenue Statement of Practice SP9/79. This declared that 'the asset resulting from the expenditure – the master print of the film – is "plant" for capital allowance purposes'. This means that films could now qualify for the 100% first-year capital allowance, thus opening the way to sale and leaseback deals: with the print being able to be written off for tax purposes, the investor was cushioned against loss. A loss-making film could still end up being profitable for him.

As a result, leaseback deals quickly became one of the most important ways of financing feature films. They were structured around a seller, a lessee and a lessor. The seller was the production company, the lessee either the distributor or the licensor of the distribution rights, and the lessor either a bank or a corporation with a high tax liability.

If a film company were to approach a bank or a corporation, asking them to invest in the film business, thus making the capital

*Laughterhouse* (dir. Richard Eyre)

allowance system available to the prospective investor, the bank would still be unlikely to get involved because, although it could claim capital allowance, there was no guarantee that it would get its investment back. At this point, the role of the lessee becomes important: by guaranteeing the bank over a fixed period of years a return equal to the sum of its original investment, it thus transfers any risk from the bank to the lessee (normally a distributor).

The difficulty in arranging such deals, however, was that the producer had to find a bank or a corporation that had money subject to a high taxation rate, and then a distributor or licensor of distribution rights to pay back the loan over a period of years. Banks would negotiate a leaseback deal only with a lessee who had a sound financial base to work from because, if the film was not successful and the lessee lost money on it, the bank still wanted assurances that it would be repaid over the stated period. Such deals, therefore, involved large companies with sufficient funds behind them to allay any fears that the bank might have had.

The Inland Revenue's policy was aimed at increasing investment in the British film industry. However, until 1982, Statement of Practice SP9/79 did not always fulfil this aim. One of the first banks to enter the film market was Barclays. In 1981, Mercantile Credit (a part of Barclays) bought a package of films from Paramount for over £40 million. These films were not, however, British made. The following year, the Inland Revenue decided to tighten the rules so that the 100% first-year capital allowance applied only to investments in British films or those with mainly British content.

Sale and leaseback deals attracted a good many merchant banks into investing in films. Chemco, a leading subsidiary of Chemical Bank, has been involved with *The Dogs of War*, *The French Lieutenant's Woman*, *Eye of the Needle* and *Local Hero* – all British films. Gail Hegarty Fell, writing in *Euromoney* in June 1983, put Chemco's total involvement in the two preceding years at £100 million, spread over nine films. Bank of America, though acting as corporate banker to several American film companies, had in the past left British films alone. In 1982, however, the Bank reviewed the whole entertainment industry and decided to develop in this direction. Manufacturer's Hanover likewise investigated the possibilities, through Robert Chris, managing director of Manufacturer's Hanover Industrial Finance Limited, pointed out one of the difficulties. He was quoted in *Euromoney* as saying: 'Even in a straightforward financing transaction, where the lender has first

class security, the problem is that the documentation required is more complex for films and definitely different from that found in an ordinary lease.'[1] Yet, he added, this might be an advantage: 'because it's difficult and complicated, there is more potential to make money out of it.'

As leaseback deals grew more complicated, there was scope for intermediaries. Albion Films Ltd., a company formed in 1981, arranges finance for films. 10% owned by Samuel Montagu (which in turn is 60% owned by the Midland Bank) and 10% owned by the ICFC – the remaining shares belong to three individuals – it acts as lessee, taking on the distribution rights, and paying a rental to the bank over a fixed period. It was, for example, the lessee for *Educating Rita*. In that instance, the structure of the deal was as follows: Acorn, the production company, financed the film by selling the master print to St Michael's Finance (a subsidiary of Marks and Spencer), which then leased the film to Albion, the distributor. The money which paid for the film to be made before there was a master print was provided by Samuel Montagu.

Some British banks have financed films on a secured lending basis. Guinness Mahon has completed 15 to 20 of these transactions over the past few years. The company is now more active than any other bank in London or even Europe, in terms of the number of deals and the total amount of financing related to the film industry.

Since the April 1984 budget, however, the situation has changed somewhat. The Government has decided to phase out capital allowances. The allowances now stand at 75%, reducing to 50% in the next fiscal year, and disappearing altogether by April 1986. When this change was announced, it created quite an outcry in the film industry, and attempts were made – unsuccessfully – to get the Government to treat film as an exception. Judging by the Government's stance on the issue, this was never likely to succeed. But

---

**Producers have to live with the times and the hard truth is that government handouts cannot realistically be made when more serious demands are made on the economy. If wailing producers would hammer more often at the doors of relatives and friends, and indeed enemies, in search of development money, their time would be better spent. I could find few takers in Britain so I moved to foreign targets to produce British films.**

**Euan Lloyd, Producer**

---

attention has also been focused on alternative areas of tax concessions which might induce financiers into the film business: the industry has, after all, a reputation for finding loopholes.

The main scheme that now appears to offer an alternative to capital allowances is the enthusiastically named Business Expansion Scheme. Under it, the maximum which one individual can invest is now £40,000. The original condition under the old business start-up scheme – that relief can be restricted to 50% of the issued share capital – has been abolished, and in general investors should be able to claim their money back from the Inland Revenue, either as a lump sum or as an adjustment to their tax coding, more quickly than before.

The Business Expansion Scheme has certainly met with a much more positive response from financial advisers than the start-up scheme (first introduced in 1981). The conditions are less complex, and it is generally felt that more people will be persuaded to put cash into established companies than into start-ups. As far as film is concerned, what is likely to happen is that, instead of the producer having to approach rich financiers individually to collect £40,000 from each, firms are being set up by companies such as Guinness

Mahon, who advertise for rich clients and thus find the investors. These companies, it is hoped, will have large sums of money to spend on high-risk investments such as films. However, getting them to part with their money is a task still left to the skills of the independent producer, who faces the same problems with these new companies as with other financial institutions. What such companies do offer, however, is a new source of finance which is potentially important for the film industry as a whole.

All in all, there would seem to be more sources of risk capital in the UK than ever before. Yet many film producers are unhappy with what the City has to offer. They complain that little interest is shown in their projects, and that, all too often, they are sent packing with scarcely a helpful or informed comment on what they are doing. No doubt fault lies on both sides. But, according to John Parkin, the industrialist who is now managing director of the venture capital organisation, English and Caledonian, many of those in search of money fail to show professionalism in their approach. Susan Lloyd of the American Capital Publishing Corporation similarly points out that many venture capitalists are not as adept at presenting themselves and preparing a business plan as their American counterparts. Consequently, it has in many cases been a very difficult process to bring potential investments to the point where a final decision can be made on their viability.

The majority of producers I spoke to in connection with this chapter had a very limited understanding of how best to raise finance from financial institutions. Those who had been successful were people with a business background who understood the needs and wants of the financier and adopted a professional approach. The days of a film producer talking a city institution into funding a film on the basis of personal charm alone are over. If films are to be considered by financiers from a professional standpoint, it is imperative that producers act with the degree of professionalism that is expected of them. All too often, we have heard how the growth of the film industry has been thwarted by the lack of financial courage shown by merchant banks, venture capitalists or independent financiers. But very little has been put forward to explain such a circumstance. It is a popular myth that the only reason for the decline in British film production is the lack of courage of financial institutions. It is an argument that fails to recognise that the film packages on offer are possibly not what the financiers want, or even that they are presented in a fashion that is

41

not acceptable to the financier. As I say, fault probably lies on both sides, but it is hard not to believe that more now rests with the producer than with the financier.

Arguments which are presented in favour of the Government playing a greater role in the financing of films generally ignore – wilfully or otherwise – the underlying cause of the lack of success of British films. Like any industry, if the product is what the consumer wants (or can be persuaded to want), the companies will not require government intervention. It is only when the product is not selling that a clamour of voices insists that the Government should give more support to an industry. The film business is one such industry, in which there is growing demand for intervention.

But no industry can survive without profit, no matter how many Government subsidies there are. And, to create a profit, it must make 'majority audience' films. Government subsidies promote films that are geared to specific audiences, and they do not benefit the shape of the industry in the long run, whatever they may do for film culture. To be successful, films must be competitive internationally, and, to be competitive internationally, films must have wide popular appeal.

The financiers I interviewed were interested in financing commercially oriented films – that is, films which could gain pre-sold distribution contracts. What was generally preferred was a portfolio of films put on offer by a management team. That is to say, a Pension Fund might invest considerable sums with a company with financial experience behind it, alongside a portfolio of films with which to spread the risk. Such companies are, at the moment, few and far between. However, if the British film industry wants to grow as an industry, it must provide financiers with the appropriate projects: that is, companies providing an experienced management team and a portfolio of films based on commercially saleable themes that are capable of achieving pre-sold distribution guarantees. Without these as a foundation, there can be no industry.

# 4

# Three companies: Boyd's Co., HandMade and Goldcrest

The history of cinema has, traditionally, been that
of its directors. But the British film industry's current state
of almost-health owes just as much to the energy
and commitment of producers and production executives.
**Robert Murphy** charts the fortunes of three of
Britain's most interesting 'independents' – Boyd's Co.,
HandMade and Goldcrest. Profiling the men
behind them, he looks at how they have been able to put
their (generally) successful packages together.

British film production, perhaps because of its very precarious-ness, has never settled into the monolithic solidity of the Hollywood studio system. The two big, vertically integrated companies which are now Rank and Thorn-EMI did have their own studios; but only for a brief period in the early 1930s did they completely dominate the production side of the industry. At all other times, they shared the market with a plethora of independent producers ranging from high-flying moguls like Alexander Korda, through reliable studio heads such as John Corfield at British National and Michael Balcon at Ealing, to fly-by-night producers of 'B' movies and 'quota quickies'. Rank's Pinewood, as much as Korda's Denham, was built to accommodate the independent producer, and most of the big films backed by the Rank Organisation in the 1940s were made by independent producers.

Though Hollywood's hegemony was, if anything, more complete in the pre-TV era than it is now, the healthiness of cinema attendance (1,635 million in 1946 compared to 64 million in 1983)

43

and the application of a compulsory quota of British films meant that a relatively large number of films were produced in Britain. From the early 1950s onwards, television gradually took over the function (and much of the personnel) of the small studios and independent producers. Decline in production was, however, cushioned by the increasing involvement of American companies freed from Hollywood by the break-up of the studio system: by 1968, nearly 90% of the films made in Britain were wholly or partly American financed. There then followed a gradual withdrawal, as it was realised that the handful of British films which had been successful in America – *Tom Jones, Georgie Girl, Alfie* – were not easily emulated, and that the atmosphere of Swinging London was no guarantee of box-office success.

This provoked something of a crisis among British producers, who had come to rely on American backing for their films. Their plight was made worse when, in August 1976, British Lion, the most important indigenous source of finance for independent producers, was taken over by EMI. Barry Spikings and Michael Deeley, British Lion's leading executives, were absorbed into EMI; and Spikings, on becoming head of production, persuaded his corporate bosses of the desirability of making films in America. While film production in Britain passed through its lowest ebb, EMI lavished millions of dollars on a string of Hollywood-style extravaganzas which, with the exception of *The Deer Hunter*, failed dismally to live up to expectations.[1]

Rank, having been absent from the field for some years, unexpectedly returned to film production in 1977, but their production programme proceeded in fits and starts and was abruptly terminated again in June 1980. A couple of extremely interesting films had emerged – Anthony Harvey's *Eagle's Wing* and Nicolas Roeg's *Bad Timing* – but they were sadly mishandled by the distribution side of the organisation and were no more successful than the predictably whimsical dross which made up the bulk of the Rank output.

The examples of, among others, the new German cinema and the Australian 'New Wave' seemed to suggest less conventional sources of finance – television companies, profit-sharing schemes, tax-shelter money. But in Britain, they were not easily tapped. Television companies did, of course, set up film-making subsidiaries – Black Lion, Euston Films, Southern Pictures – but they were largely concerned with producing TV films and series, and made only infrequent ventures into feature film production. Lew Grade's ITC made a more substantial intervention but its policy of putting together internationally attractive big-budget films which could be substantially financed by pre-sales in foreign markets had little relevance for independent British producers. It was not until the advent of Channel 4 that the latter were able to turn to television as an important source of finance for features.

Government policy has been discouragingly arbitrary. In 1978, reports issued forth from both the Prime Minister's Working Party and the Interim Action Committee (then headed by National Film Finance Corporation Chairman, Sir John Terry), recommending the establishment of a British Film Authority and calling on the Government to take a more active role in the affairs of the film industry. The appointment of Mamoun Hassan, an independent film-maker who had run the British Film Institute Production Board between 1971 and 1974, as Sir John's successor at the NFFC appeared to signal the Government's good faith, and there was general expectation that the NFFC's debts would be written off and that it would be granted a new and substantial pool of capital. The election, in 1979, of a Tory Government committed to the mass slaughter of quangoes and lame ducks rather dented these ambitious hopes. The NFFC was given permanent funding, but on a very small scale (20% of the Eady Levy or £1.5 million, whichever should be greater). With the continuing decline in cinema admissions, the sum has never exceeded £1.5 million. Though Hassan has been able to do useful work backing films – *The Duellists*, *Babylon*, *Gregory's Girl*, *Loose Connections* – which otherwise would probably not have been made, the NFFC has not been able to act on a large enough scale to make any significant impact on the economic structure of the industry. Its future, as a privatised British Screen Finance Corporation, seems uncertain.

Fortunately, however, producers have not proved entirely incapable of self-help. In 1976, a group of young film-makers, dissatisfied with the staid and conservative British Producers Association, formed the Association of Independent Producers. It was soon functioning as a vigorous pressure group and as a forum for debate and self-enlightenment for producers and directors operating on the precarious peripheries of the industry, many of whom – David Puttnam, Alan Parker, Clive Parsons and Davina Belling, Simon Perry – were to become commercially successful over the next few years. In March 1978, Richard Craven, AIP Chairman, and Simon Perry set up the First Investors Film Management Company as a non-profitmaking film finance company. It attracted considerable attention and support – the idea was that the films should be economically budgeted and that creative personnel should be persuaded to take small salaries and a percentage of the films' profits. But it foundered on the problem of acquiring a convincing package of developed scripts. However, Craven and Perry did at least show that sources outside the film industry – the American Express company among others – could be interested in putting money into British films.

The problem was to find ways of ̈making such investment genuinely attractive. In America, Canada, Australia, Japan and Germany, money has, since the early 1970s, been channelled into film production less for its inherent profitability than to take advantage of tax avoidance schemes. Britain's tax system, however, seemed less pliable than most and there was no major intrusion of tax shelter money into the film industry such as that brought by companies like Geria, IFV (Cinema 77), CIP Filmproduktion, Cinerenta and Palladium in Germany, which together provided £34 million for film production in 1978. However, Roy Tucker and Ron Plummer's Rossminster group of companies, which, during its brief

Toyah Willcox in *The Tempest* (Boyd's Co.)

career, is estimated to have cost the Inland Revenue £200 million, did invest a small amount in British film production. The main beneficiary was a programme of films set up by the young producer/ director Don Boyd.

## Boyd's Co.

Boyd's rash dynamism had taken him from film school to a full-length feature film, *Intimate Reflections* (1974), within three years. Despite the film's moderate performance at the box office, Boyd went on to make *East of Elephant Rock* (1976), and to set up a package of five low-budget films on which he proposed to act as executive producer. He was fortunate in attracting the attention of Rossminster's Roy Tucker who, no doubt aware of the prevalence of tax-shelter film finance elsewhere, agreed to find the money. A scheme was devised whereby high-rate taxpayers were able to buy into a series of limited partnerships which would, legally, allow them tax losses around four times as great as what they had paid in – the high 'gearing' on which such deals stand or fall. For example, twenty-six individuals who paid in £369,750 were able to claim tax losses of £1.5 million.[2]

Of the five films, *Scum* was highly successful in Britain but disappointingly received in America; *The Tempest* was a huge critical success, but an expensive marketing campaign designed to widen its appeal beyond the art-house audience meant that it was slow to show a profit; *Sweet William* did poorly at the box-office, though losses were partly covered by a distribution deal with ITC; and *Blue Suede Shoes* and *Hussie* fared badly all round (though the latter acquired a cult following in America because of Helen Mirren's performance). The package as a whole, which cost little more than £1.3 million, just about broke even, thanks to subsequent cable TV sales. Boyd's company was paid a fee for its production services and Tucker's investors were happy enough with the tax advantages gained from their paper losses not to worry about the meagreness of the profits that eventually trickled in.

Tax shelter schemes are still possible; but, in September 1979, the murky waters in which Rossminster operated were clarified by a government ruling that investment in film production could be written off against tax in the year the film was made rather than over a period deemed to be the useful life of the film. This was a far more straightforward tax advantage, and it has proved an incentive to institutional investors – banks, pension funds, investment trusts,

47

insurance companies – to involve themselves in film production – until, that is, Chancellor Nigel Lawson announced in his 1984 budget that he would phase them out.

Boyd and veteran producer Michael Relph attempted to persuade Barry Spikings that EMI should back their next package of films, pointing out the low risks involved in producing economically budgeted pictures, the more lucrative returns on foreign sales which could be expected from EMI's international distribution set-up, and the prestige value of supporting indigenous British films. Spikings, however, preferred to take one of Boyd's projects – a medium budget road movie – and ask him to produce it as part of EMI's programme of Hollywood type films. This led to Boyd's absence in America for virtually two years making the $24 million *Honky-Tonk Freeway*, the losses on which would have covered the budget of Boyd's package of British films several times over.

Boyd's most recent project, *Gossip*, which he began shooting in October 1982, had to be abandoned when his financial backers – Raymond Lanciault and Alan Shephard, purporting to represent a £1,000 million trust fund, the Martini Foundation – failed to produce the money.[3] Significantly, the other two films made by Boyd's company since his return from America – *An Unsuitable Job for a Woman* and *Scrubbers* – have been financed, not by tax shelter investors, but by production companies who have their own financial resources, Goldcrest and HandMade.

## HandMade

HandMade Films, was set up in 1978 as a partnership between George Harrison and Euroatlantic, the company controlled by Harrison's financial adviser, Denis O'Brien. Its purpose was specifically to make the Monty Python movie, *Life of Brian*, which had been developed with backing from EMI but then shelved as too controversial. The film was extremely successful, and HandMade agreed to back individual Python projects. Eric Idle was given money to develop a script based on the Gilbert and Sullivan operetta, *Pirates of Penzance*, but HandMade then rejected it as too expensive to be commercially viable. Terry Gilliam, who had already made the visually impressive *Jabberwocky* for £600,000, was considered a better risk, and HandMade agreed to put up the £1.5 million (eventually £2.5 million) for *Time Bandits*.

Gilliam's achievement in producing a sci-fi fantasy on such a moderate budget was remarkable, but it involved him in extensive post-production work creating his own special effects. The film was only moderately successful in Britain and attracted little attention from the American majors. But both Gilliam and O'Brien were convinced that it had the potential to attract a large American audience. Mini-major Avco-Embassy was persuaded to distribute the film with HandMade guaranteeing costs to the extent of $5.5 million and bringing in their own team to supervise the marketing campaign. The gamble paid off, and *Time Bandits* finally grossed over $18 million, making it the most successful British film of 1981 after the Oscar winning *Chariots of Fire*. But an acrimonious dispute arose over the distribution of the profits. Gilliam considered he was ill rewarded for all the extra work he had done on the

---

**British cinema has for decades been riven by an endless and largely sterile debate revolving around the notion of 'art' versus 'commerce'. Recently it has become clear that this argument formed extremely convenient cover for fundamental creative inadequacies on *both* sides.**

**Our job in the UK is to set about defining 'British' pictures in the broadest possible terms. Our cinema can and must reflect a genuine *creative* perspective. It must reflect the desire to see Britain and the world through British eyes and attitudes, and to *communicate* what we see in an entertaining and comprehensive manner to audiences around the world; where cinematic images and stereotypes 'haunt the unconscious'.**

**David Puttnam, Producer**

---

film; and O'Brien felt that the risks HandMade had taken in virtually distributing the film themselves in America together with the heavy interest charges they had incurred during the long post-production schedule were insufficiently acknowledged.

Perhaps inevitably with a young and unconventional company, HandMade have been through a series of mistakes and false starts. Their attempt at conventional commercial distribution – buying in exploitation films like *The Burning, Tattoo* and *Venom* – misfired, and they have subsequently dispensed with a distribution set-up needing to be fed with outside product. Their present strategy involves bringing in outside publicity and advertising agencies to collaborate on the marketing and distribution of their own films, a technique which proved very successful with *The Missionary*.

On the production side, disputes with individual members of the

*A Private Function* (HandMade)

HAPPY WEDDING DAY

Python team have highlighted the dangers of acting as a service agency for Python projects, and HandMade has subsequently extended the range of talent upon which it can draw. The ambitiousness of Idle's *Pirates of Penzance*, Graham Chapman's *Yellowbeard* – on which extensive pre-production work was done before it was shunted off to the American Orion company – and Gilliam's lavish fantasy *Brazil* – made in 1984 with backing from 20th Century-Fox – would have involved HandMade in a Hollywood-scale production programme which was beyond the scope of its financial resources. Instead, they have decided on a policy of making low to medium budget films not exclusively dependent on Python talent, including *Water*, written by Dick Clement (who also directed) and Ian La Frenais (who produced); *A Private Function*, written by Alan Bennett, directed by Malcolm Mowbray and produced by Mark Shivas; and *Travelling Men*, written by Peter McDougall, directed by John MacKenzie and produced by Ray Cooper.

This will eventually entail the company looking beyond the personal fortunes of its partners. But O'Brien is insistent that HandMade's control over its films will remain untrammelled and that there will be no move towards 'safe' methods and 'safe' subjects. 'We do try to bet with every film – as opposed to the normal practice whereby a producer puts a film together, includes a very high fee for himself and raises the budget by doing as many advance deals as possible. That way, everybody takes their cash out on day one and nobody cares if the film is successful. We do just the opposite. We only make money if the film is successful.'[4]

It is an attitude which is very attractive to film-makers. And the fact that Palace Pictures was able to secure the financial backing of the Norwich Union group for its unconventional distribution activities and that Lewis Gilbert's Acorn Pictures were funded by the Prudential to make *Educating Rita* and *Not Quite Jerusalem* suggests that conservative City institutions are now more ready to become involved. Much depends though on the fate of the very large scale City investment in the Goldcrest group of companies.

*Goldcrest*
Goldcrest was the brainchild of Jake Eberts, a Canadian chemical engineer turned merchant banker. It was formally established in November 1976 as a film development company attempting to tap the 'strong market demand for good quality feature films for adult and family entertainment which do not depend on explicit sex or violence for their audience appeal.'[5] Eberts first began to dabble in film finance back in 1974, when he borrowed $50,000 from a group of associates to develop an animated feature film, *Watership Down*. He then approached various financial institutions with the intention of raising the £1.2 million necessary to get the film into production. Two of the most receptive sources were the publishing conglomerate Pearson-Longman and the investment trust Electra House. The commercial success of *Watership Down* led Pearson-Longman to suggest to Eberts, at this time Managing Director of the Oppenheimer merchant bank, that he set up a film development fund of £250,000 to which they and Electra House would each contribute 50%.

Working on a small-scale, part-time basis, Eberts provided the backing for Ken Loach and Tony Garnett to develop *Black Jack*, which was then sold to the NFFC, and for Clive Parsons and Davina Belling to develop *Breaking Glass*, which was sold to Allied Stars, a new company set up by Egyptian shipping magnate Dodi Fayed. Goldcrest's advance of £30,000 for *Breaking Glass* was repaid, plus a fee of £25,000 and a share of the profits. The package was sufficiently commercial to attract enough pre-sales to cover its costs but not so successful at the box office as to bring in extensive profits. Both parties were happy enough with the deal, though, and Allied Stars agreed to provide 50% of the finance (the other 50%

51

coming from 20th Century-Fox) for a Goldcrest project developed by Colin Welland and David Puttnam – *Chariots of Fire*.

With development proving successful, Eberts was able to persuade his financial backers to make a more substantial commitment in the form of finance for film production. Before settling in England, Eberts had spent three years in New York as an investment banker setting up and supporting small business ventures. In view of the still sickly state of health of film production in Britain, it was considered advisable to utilise Eberts' American connections and set up a film finance company in New York. By December 1978 he had succeeded in attracting sufficient support to set up International Film Investors with a capital of $10 million, $1 million of which came from Pearson-Longman and Electra House.

Throughout 1979, as IFI attempted to set up deals on a programme of American films (*Hopscotch, Escape from New York, The Howling*), Eberts set about raising a sister fund of capital in Britain. In July 1980, he was able to announce that he had managed to raise £8.2 million from various institutional investors including the merchant bankers Noble Grossart, Murray Johnstone and Schroder Wagg, the National Union of Miners Pension Fund, Electra House and Pearson-Longman (which now assumed a controlling interest). This new and very substantial pool of finance was vested in a limited partnership, Goldcrest Films International, and was to be used to invest in six to eight films annually in co-operation with IFI (one of the projects developed by IFI was Richard Attenborough's *Gandhi*). With measured caution, Eberts announced that, 'wherever possible, Goldcrest will invest in films for which a substantial part of the budget is covered by theatrical or television pre-sales or by distribution guarantees'.[6]

Eberts' success, both in raising capital and in investing it wisely, opened up the prospect of a large-scale operation. Until May 1981, Goldcrest had operated with only two part-time employees, Eberts and an assistant; IFI had been run by Eberts' American partner, Josiah Child. Now, with the enthusiastic support of James Lee, the new Chief Executive of Pearson-Longman, Eberts set about raising additional capital and recruiting a team of people capable of organising a Goldcrest production and marketing operation which would, in addition, expand beyond feature film production into television. By August 1981, Mike Wooller had been coaxed from his position as head of documentaries at Thames to become Managing Director of the TV division of what had become Goldcrest Films and Television. Pearson-Longman agreed to set up a separate pool of £5.5 million for TV production and a discreet canvassing of institutional investors by Edinburgh merchant bankers Noble Grossart brought in another £9.4 million.[7]

By the middle of 1983, Goldcrest had over 40 employees and a capital base of £26 million. *Gandhi*, its first major British investment, was proving hugely successful, while lesser successes were being marked up by *Local Hero*, *The Ploughman's Lunch*, and one of the 'First Love' series of films Goldcrest made for Channel 4, *Experience Preferred (But Not Essential)*. Eberts, however, seems to have become increasingly dissatisfied with his role in the company and at the end of November announced that he would be leaving to head the London office of the American mini-major, Embassy Communications. With Lord Grade, he is to organise a European production programme for Embassy. James Lee resigned his position with Pearson-Longman to become Goldcrest's Chief Executive and a thorough reorganisation of Goldcrest's complex structure of partnerships was promised. At the beginning of 1984, Sandy Lieberson was appointed head of production.

Lieberson, an ex-agent with the William Morris agency and Creative Media Associates, has worked in England since the mid-1960s. Though an American, he has played an active role in

Ben Kingsley in *Gandhi*

British film production. After producing *Performance*, he formed a partnership with David Puttnam called Goodtimes Enterprises, and, between 1971 and 1976, turned out a series of interestingly diverse films, including *The Pied Piper*, *That'll Be the Day*, *The Double Headed Eagle*, *The Final Programme*, *Mahler*, *Stardust*, *Lisztomania* and *Bugsy Malone*. After Puttnam's departure for America to work on *Midnight Express*, Lieberson produced Terry Gilliam's *Jabberwocky* and was then invited by friend and fellow agent Alan Ladd Jr. to head 20th Century-Fox's European opera-

---

**These days just about everybody, it seems, is on automatic pilot when it comes to windy declarations about how British film-making, after years of getting its knees dusty, is back on its feet and is once again swaggering around the international market place like some land counterpart of Drake's navy. The truth of the matter is that although the present level of film production induces confidence, it probably won't lead to much beyond parochial self-congratulation until film-makers begin to acknowledge that their films need an audience outside of a home market in which cinemagoing is largely a moribund habit. Britain could be producing the most exciting and uncompromising films anywhere at the moment: its skills, imagination and independent-spiritedness are constant evidence of the probability. But if the industry is to flourish, it must look beyond this country in subject, treatment, style. Not to Hollywood, where most films still seem under-considered and over-budgeted; and certainly not to the idea of mid-Atlantic cinema, which prompted so many disastrous films of so little character. But there is a world out there. And really, it's about time we noticed it.**

**Al Clark, Virgin Films**

---

tions. When Ladd left Fox in June 1979 to form his own company, Lieberson replaced him as President. He was able to put *The Janitor*, *Nine to Five* and *Chariots of Fire* into production before the backwash of the David Begelman scandal deposited Alan Hirschfield and a bevy of Columbia executives at Fox. Unsurprisingly, Lieberson teamed up again with Ladd, becoming European representative of the Ladd Company, where he supervised the production of such big-budget pictures as *Outland*, *Blade Runner* and *Once Upon a Time in America*.

Though he retains close links with Hollywood and expresses no special brief for British films, Lieberson – an ardent supporter of the AIP and the NFFC – is respected by a wide spectrum of British film-makers. He is enthusiastic about the infusion of new talent into the industry, but aware of the danger of fashion rather than ability dictating who makes films. 'It is important that we don't turn our back on the really fine talent in this country and elsewhere that is of an older generation. They still have a lot to contribute. I think it would be a great mistake to rule them out just because they're over fifty. I'm going to be over fifty myself soon and I don't want ruling out.'

In June 1980, *Screen Digest*, a multi-media marketing journal, complained that 'the part of the film industry in Britain which has its roots in the cinema (viz. feature films) is so outmoded in its attitudes that there is only one way for it to go: down. This is not merely a reflection of our view about the social and technical changes that will depress the cinema industry, but also a comment on the inflexible people who run that industry.' Four years later, there are few of those 'inflexible people' left in control of the industry. The development of ancillary markets and the greater receptivity of American distributors to British films has attracted new finance and new talent into the industry and has opened up

The Killing Fields

opportunities for British films which companies such as Boyd's Co., HandMade and Goldcrest have consciously attempted to grasp.

The future of theatrical exhibition in Britain is, of course, far from secure but there are signs that the big cinema chains are at last beginning to emulate the London independents in seeking to provide comfortable, well-programmed cinemas. However, the returns from the British market will continue to cover the costs of only the smallest-budgeted movies and overseas distribution remains vitally important.

Fortunately, British films seem to have secured a small but permanent place in the American market. Distributors like the Goldwyn company have shown that the art-house market can be a lucrative one and that British films particularly those like *Chariots of Fire, Betrayal* and *Educating Rita*, which are ostentatiously British, are as acceptable there as traditional European art movies. Bigger budgeted films like Goldcrest's *The Killing Fields* and Thorn-EMI's *A Passage to India* have shown themselves as successful as their American counterparts on the commercial circuits. Thus there is, at last, a possibility of British films proving profitable enough to encourage further investment and of the cycle of crises which has plagued the industry finally being broken.

# 5

# But is it cinema?

It is still true to say that the best British films are to be found on TV? **Martyn Auty** acclaims the arrival of the made-for-TV film and applauds television for belatedly paying its debts to the cinema, but wonders whether the prosperous state of TV film-making threatens the art of cinema.

The argument here is nothing new. That 'British film-making is alive and well and living in television' has been self-evident for more than a decade. What is different is that in the 1980s television has begun to look outward, towards subsidising the big screen and its infant medium, video.

TV still provides a sanctuary for the film-maker who can't find commercial backers outside to take a risk on 'controversial' or 'artistic' projects, still finds work for film-makers caught between theatrical features. But recent signs suggest TV has also begun belatedly to care about the future of its elder brother medium, the cinema.

TV's initiative to begin repayment of the debt owed to cinema – thirty years of cheap, high ratings programming – came principally from Channel 4, whose Chief Executive, Jeremy Isaacs, pledged his new channel to helping reinvigorate British film-making two years before the channel went on air in November 1982. The disarmingly simple notion at Channel 4 was that the channel would either fund *in toto* or co-finance a range of film productions which would each be given a crack at the theatrical market before appearing on television.

Britain's film community could hardly believe its ears at the start of the 1980s: TV to fund cinema, instead of stealing its talent and product? But Channel 4's pledge was realised and twenty movies emerged in the first year of 'Film on Four', eight of which achieved some measure of theatrical release in the period 1982–84 while another ten made frequent appearances in subsidised cinemas like the BFI's Regional Film Theatres. One film, *The Draughtsman's Contract*, even topped the London box-office poll during a delirious period in 1983. The public was paying money to see films in the cinema which were destined for 'free' TV screenings only months later.

Other television companies took up the initiative, though to date only Central Independent Television, through its creation of a separate film-making subsidiary called Zenith, has broken through the barrier dividing TV from theatrical film exhibition. Yet a 'film arm' exists at Thames TV under the name Euston Films and the BBC has instituted a working party to investigate the possibilities of making films for cinema first and TV transmission second.

To understand the background to this radical rapprochement between the once inimical media, we need to look back, briefly, to the preceding decade. In the late 1960s and throughout the 1970s, virtually all Britain's best known producers and directors were to be found in television companies, predominantly within the BBC, but also at Granada, Thames and London Weekend. The roll call of these years is impressive: Ken Loach, Tony Garnett, Jack Gold, Michael Apted, Mike Hodges, Alan Clarke, Kenith Trodd, Stephen Frears, Mike Leigh, Karel Reisz, Alan Parker, Mark Shivas, Graham Benson, Franc Roddam, Roland Joffe, Jim Goddard, Richard Eyre, Margaret Matheson, and so on.

What this diverse group of film-makers shared, I would argue, was a passion for film as film; a concern for the celluloid medium that would not be compromised by the economic arguments within television which decreed film to be too costly for 'drama'. These were and are people who go to the movies and relate intuitively to the aesthetic values that are unique to cinema. Not that their best work for the small screen would always bear scrutiny on the big screen. Inevitably it wouldn't, because the conception of each film arose from the impulse to reach domestic audiences on screens no

58

wider than 26 inches. But on the level of 'texture', detail, editing and, in many cases, performances, this great wealth of work had the 'feel' of cinema, albeit scaled-down to TV.

Everyone from reviewers through publicists to viewers – and often the film-makers themselves – fought shy of the term TV movies/films but that was, indeed still is, what these works of between 75 and 110 minutes represent. The reticence over terminology is understandable. Around the time the BBC was pioneering one-off 'dramas on film' (late 1960s), Hollywood launched 'the TV movie'. The latter, an unjustly maligned genre, nevertheless appeared to short-change film fans with a deadeningly formulaic approach to small-screen movie-making. (It is still instructive and germane to this argument, however, to note the work of Wicking and Vahimagi in their 1978 book *The American Vein*.)[1] Of course it didn't matter what the TV film-makers called their own work generically, but their origins in departments of 'Drama' or 'Plays' and the persistence of television executives and publicists in using the word 'play' has done irreparable damage to the public's perception of such works and to the institutional politics of television companies where literary and theatrical traditions vie with graphic and cinematic thinking under the broken umbrella of 'drama'.

59

Something more tangible than terminology and ideology continues to pose problems for TV film-makers seeking theatrical outlets for their work. The craft unions within television, as distinct from those in the film industry (though many ITV staff belong to the same trade union as feature film workers) have necessarily evolved their own principles and working practices to safeguard jobs in-house and are understandably reluctant to see 'TV' films crewed by 'outside' or freelance members. This situation clearly has advantages and disadvantages: in-house technicians rising through the ranks and benefiting from several excellent training schemes should have the opportunities to work on major productions like feature-length TV films. Yet producers and directors need the freedom to handpick the best crew available for the job.

The regulations under which such films may be made are currently the agreements with the British Film and Television Producers Association (BFTPA) and the Independent Television Companies Association (ITCA). The essence of these agreements, known familiarly as 'the films agreement' and 'the television agreement', governs film-making in Britain today. In principle, BFTPA admits of freelance crewing and is the commonest agreement in use for films. It is also generally more expensive than the ITCA agreement, which is basically an in-house ITV deal between management and unions allowing for film-making in television companies. An independent television company seeking to make feature-length films for TV only transmission will use the ITCA agreement, whereas the BFTPA agreement covers all theatrical features and Films on Four. Within these agreements, 'local' deals are sometimes made in individual television companies depending on the nature of the project and its intended distribution.

Clearly this is a problematic area that is unlikely to be resolved in the short-term. The line of demarcation between TV and film is holding, in this respect at least, for the foreseeable future.

If television's new-found concern for a healthy cinema industry is to be taken seriously, and I suggest it should, it cannot be evaluated solely in terms of the aesthetic tastes of those film-makers working within the medium. A more pragmatic issue is at stake here: namely the kudos a theatrical release delivers to a film when it turns up on TV. This argument should not be underestimated. When the BBC screened *Chariots of Fire* in December 1984 the viewing figures of 14.3 million testified to the potency of that film's circuit reputation.

*Chariots* was an 'event' movie in every sense: a film score that found its way into the record collections of those who had yet to see the film; a rare occasion in film history when the names of producer and writer were known by people who normally pay no attention to credits; and, even rarer, a British Oscar winner which threw the spotlight of the popular press on to the native film industry. The film arrived on TV to a fanfare and there can be little doubt its subsequent screenings will reap ratings.

Similarly, though to a lesser degree, the two screenings Channel 4 has so far given to *The Draughtsman's Contract* have drawn considerable benefit from the 'buzz' that accompanied the film's theatrical release in London and provincial art houses. This latter

---

**Traditionally fiction film has been perceived within British broadcasting as 'the play'. Many fine films were produced but the notion of theatrical exhibition rarely even considered. Channel 4 took a different view from the outset. A relationship has developed during the last four years, suspicions have been in the main dispelled and a healthy partnership is being established between the TV and cinema industries.**

**David Rose, Senior Commissioning Editor, Channel 4**

---

case is, of course, the more honourable of the two examples since Channel 4 had *invested* in *The Draughtsman's Contract*, whereas the BBC had simply purchased *Chariots* at the going rate for feature films. Yet Channel 4 earned revenue from both forms of exhibition. It is now no longer inconceivable that a film wholly or partly produced with TV money can make its costs back before TV transmission. What follows, therefore, in viewing figures and advertising revenue is bunce.

Not every attempt in the sphere of theatrical release has worked in Channel 4's favour, however. *Giro City*, one of the earliest 'Films on Four' to go theatrical ran a miserable three weeks in a London art house. *Remembrance* suffered even greater ignominy, opening and closing within a week and David Puttnam's bid to squeeze theatrical life out of two pictures, *P'Tang, Yang, Kipperbang* and *Those Glory, Glory Days, after* their TV exposure was a lamentable failure, even by his own admission. Either the public didn't fancy the subject matter of these films, or they'd noted the advance publicity/on-air trailers and simply waited for the films to turn up on TV, or, in the case of the two Puttnam pictures, they'd already seen them and once was enough. More fundamentally perhaps, these films were perceived as small-screen films that exerted no pull on the purse strings in an age when going to the cinema was an expensive and occasional leisure pursuit. Whatever the case, judgment was duly made and Channel 4 switched its film policy towards investing in more obviously theatrical movies. Films like *The Company of Wolves* and *Paris Texas* became the recipients of funding that, a year or two earlier, would have gone into *some* of the more domestic dramas in the first two seasons on 'Film on Four'. With the creation of 'Film Four International' Channel 4 hauled itself into a bigger league of film producers, forging partnerships with European and American production companies in order to boost its film flagship slot with product that was emphatically to be seen first in the cinema and thereafter on TV. Zenith's investment in the Nicolas Roeg film *Insignificance* is of a similar order, likewise David Hare's *Wetherby*.

It now becomes clear that we are witnessing the parallel development of two strands of film-making in the area of TV/film collaboration: the first, theatrical but part-financed by television; the second tailor-made for the small screen. The problem remains whether TV is an adequate medium for such product. In a television interview

The Company of Wolves

in December 1983, the painter David Hockney remarked of a range of 'Films on Four', 'the pictures just aren't good enough when seen on TV.' If the images are inadequate, in Hockney's terms, it is hardly surprising that TV film-making leans heavily on the script and often favours the 'false image' afforded by costume drama. Especially since TV sound, too, has a long way to go before it attains the high fidelity of the best cinema sound-tracking. When every home has a wall-sized screen and quadrophonic sound, such aesthetic problems should be resolved and by then cinemas, as places of entertainment, would seem to be technologically – if not socially – obsolete.

This begs the question of whether a film proper can be defined only by the conditions of viewing. With television, the preconditions for 'pure' cinema are absent: scale is drastically reduced, instead of a darkened auditorium we have the well-lit living room, and, perhaps most crucially, the audience is individuated, an aspect readily perceived in comedy and horror films, for example. A cinema movie is as much defined by audience perception as by the author's conception, but in television it is the latter that predominates.

Furthermore, in a cinema movie the sounds and images relate to the 'world' of the film first and only secondly to the world outside. But in television, where films are produced to be slotted into an evening's schedule also comprising news, game shows, documentaries, etc., directors are encouraged to favour the outside world over the film's 'own world'. Hence the tendency of TV film-making to favour naturalism over other modes of address. When one thinks of the major British TV films of the last two decades, it is invariably the work of directors like Loach, Garnett, Joffe, that comes to mind: social realism remains the most visible profile of TV film-making.

The persistence of this tradition has clearly encouraged a set of expectations in the minds of the viewing public: that TV delivers naturalism and cinema properly remains the realm of fantasy.

The principal strength of made-for-TV films lies in their ability to address specifically domestic issues, as against home-produced theatrical films which need to keep one eye on the overseas market. Hence British television films are invariably more inclined to confront questions, social and/or political, which are also raised in theatre, literature and the press. Furthermore, because TV can respond more swiftly to current trends or events owing to a quicker turnaround in production schedules, made-for-TV films generally have a more contemporary context than their cinema counterparts.

Given the groundbed of work conventionally identified as 'Loach-Garnett' (but also involving producers like Kenith Trodd and writers like Dennis Potter, Trevor Griffiths and Jim Allen), it remains true that 'social' themes in TV drama are highly regarded by TV executives and highly prized at international television festivals. The success[2] in 1984 of a quartet of films by David Leland for Central Television endorses the prominence of a tradition that can be traced back to the 'Loach-Garnett' era. Produced by Margaret Matheson, the four films (*Birth of a Nation, Flying into the Wind, Made in Britain* and *R.H.I.N.O.*) effectively rejuvenated the earlier tradition by focusing on the lives of young people in the bleak years of mass unemployment and the consequent breakdown of a social structure formerly thought to be inviolate. The work of the writer G. F. Newman (*Law and Order, The Nation's Health*) can also be seen to sharpen the 'Loach-Garnett' thrust into a searing attack on British institutions (respectively the police and the health service) which raises urgent questions about the day-to-day 'management' of people's lives.

Inevitably, in this context, the social/political situation in Northern Ireland has served as a focus for such arguments (though it must be said that British film-makers on the whole have failed to address the question of the war in Ireland as acutely as, for example, the French tackled the Algerian War in the 1960s). None the less, the recent film by Mike Leigh, *Four Days in July* marks a new approach to the films-about-Ireland genre in so far as it is based not on a pre-existing text (as with *Cal*) but on research and conversations and improvisations with the local community and local actors in Belfast. The film has a dramatic honesty far greater than any tractarian piece about the struggle between the two communities in the troubled city of Belfast.

Indeed the work of Mike Leigh, essentially rooted in experimental theatre in the later 1960s/early 70s, has become one of the major landmarks of British film-making in the last decade. Leigh constructs his dramas out of detailed improvisation to create a unique authenticity of character and situation – hence the screen credit 'devised and directed by Mike Leigh'. In recent years *Grown Ups* (1980), *Meantime* (1982) and *Fours Days in July* (1984) have consolidated Leigh's reputation as the keenest analyst of the

Four Days in July (BBC)

contemporary anguish felt, but rarely voiced, by the most oppressed sector of the population. Criticisms of Leigh range from those bemoaning the 'loss' of the humour for which he was celebrated in plays like *Abigail's Party* to those which assert that his distinctive mode of reprepresentation shows but does not argue the political subtexts of his drama. None the less his is a remarkable body of work, some of which has been shown theatrically overseas but is specifically devised for the small screen medium.

It follows from earlier remarks about the 'domesticity' of made-for-TV films that subject matter relating to 'regional' or 'provincial' areas represents an important strand in British TV film-making. There is, of course, a primary problem of definition in this matter: namely whether one is referring to parts of Great Britain or separate countries with their own native film traditions. TV confuses the issue further since some of the work in question emanates from 'regional' centres of national organisations like the BBC, whilst other films spring independently from a local context where nationalism of one kind or another underpins the culture (e.g. Scotland and Wales).

Without doubt the most prominent aspect of this work has emerged from Scotland where the native film culture had been held down for years by a combination of underfunding and official mismanagement but received an enormous impetus with the advent of Channel 4. It was hardly surprising that Scotland would be well favoured by Channel 4 since the channel's Chief Executive, Jeremy Isaacs, was Scottish-born and had produced a seminal film, *A Sense of Freedom*, for Scottish Television only a year before he took the

*Giro City* (Channel 4)

reins of the new channel. The film is based on the autobiography of Jimmy Boyle, originally serving a series of life sentences for murder, who becomes self-rehabilitated in the course of his confinement in the progressive Special Unit at Barlinnie Prison in Glasgow. The hard-edged quality of writer Peter MacDougall's production was typical of the same writer's work for BBC Scotland, notably *Just a Boy's Game* and *Just Another Saturday*. MacDougall subsequently transposed this style to non-Scottish subjects.

Scotland also provided the setting for a handful of Films on Four which treated subject matter both urban (*Living Apart Together*) and rural (*Hero; Another Time, Another Place; Ill Fares the Land*). But it was always more than mere 'setting'. *Hero*, for example, was the product of many years spent by director Barney Platts-Mills living in a remote part of Western Scotland, researching and rehearsing with local people the historic and legendary adventures of Dermid O'Duinne and Finn McCool. *Hero* was a notorious first for British cinema: the only film made wholly in Gaelic, a factor which severely debilitated its reception with both press and public; but the initiative to produce work from within emphatically non-English culture is none the less notable.

*Ill Fares the Land* is a more conventional work, retelling in dramatic form the story of the evacuation of the island of St Kilda and the consequent loss of a separate lifestyle that had sustained the St Kildan community for centuries. Close in form and theme to an earlier tradition of British cinema, perhaps best exemplified by Michael Powell's *Edge of the World* (1937), *Ill Fares the Land* looked strangely old-fashioned and out of touch on its TV transmission.

Wales has been less well represented as a film culture, with only Karl Francis's *Giro City* achieving any theatrical exposure (and that very limited) prior to TV transmission. The strongest aspect of *Giro City* is the analysis of a depressed community in South Wales threatened by industrial expansion and its accompanying corruption, but the film was accounted a critical failure for its attempts to turn social realism into thriller via the device of a journalistic exposé.

Broader political themes of a national and international nature remain curiously infrequent in British TV drama despite their obvious potential in foreign television markets, though it should be noted that the TV series or mini-series often operates in this area (e.g. *Jewel in the Crown, Kennedy, Wynne and Penkovsky*, etc.).

The high cost of producing TV films abroad also goes some way to accounting for the rareness of big international political films. It is, for example, tacitly admitted by Thames Television that their Film on Four *Saigon, Year of the Cat* written by David Hare and directed by Stephen Frears would have been more effective if executed on the scale on which it was conceived – a 'mini-epic' about the fall and evacuation of Saigon at the end of the Vietnam War – rather than scaled down to TV proportions and budgets. More successful TV films on political themes (albeit somewhat obliquely represented) are Stephen Poliakoff's *Soft Targets*, the story of a Soviet diplomat in London, and Alan Bennett's *An Englishman Abroad*, a dramatisation of the real-life meeting between the actress Coral Browne and the spy Guy Burgess in Moscow in 1958. The latter film, directed by John Schlesinger (returning to television for the first time in seventeen years), is one of the finest British films, cinema or TV, in the last ten years, treating aspects of the British political conscience with a subtle, humorous yet disturbing resonance.

To some extent the paucity of political subject matter in British independent film is a misconception. The work exists, as Sheila Whitaker argues in a later chapter, but it is either curiously invisible or resolutely parochial. Again Channel 4 has bravely sought to remedy the situation by its contribution to the 'Workshops Declaration', a deal struck between the major craft union, ACTT, and the BFI whereby films produced by BFI-funded regional film workshops would be guaranteed television exhibition on Channel 4 in programme slots under the banner title 'The Eleventh Hour'. This marks an important step towards greater accessibility for low-budget, drama and documentary of an agit-prop or confrontationalist nature.

Among the workshops who have made consistent and cogent films for their own communities and for the 'Eleventh Hour' are Amber Films, based on Tyneside, Chapter in Cardiff, and the East Midlands workshop. The London-based Cinema Action group have also been active in developing a wider role for the exhibition of films that challenge the predominant TV documentary tradition with its impedimenta of centrist bias and 'balance'. But the persistent problem with workshop output is that of preaching to the converted and it is hard to escape the feeling that they represent a sop to the collective conscience of the BFI, ACTT and Channel 4 by maintaining a tradition of independent film-making long after the

Alan Bates in *An Englishman Abroad* (BBC)

audiences for such work have disappeared. To this it should be added that there persists within the BFI a resentment that the Institute's commitment to the workshops has progressively drained resources from the Production Board to the point where the BFI can fund only one or two feature-length productions per year.

As a general rule television prefers to generate its own polemical programming rather than seek it in the communities where 'struggle' in the keenly political sense engenders its distinctive modes of expression. It is frankly unrealistic to imagine that a network of regional film workshops will grow into a reckonable 'circuit' of alternative cinemas because of Channel 4's 'Eleventh Hour' initiative. Indeed, it seems far more likely that workshop product will find its audiences more or less exclusively on Channel 4.

If television retains the upper hand in British film-making in the 1980s, it is partly due to the fact that TV's corporate structures and in-house facilities permit a faster turnaround of product and a consequently greater output. The question remains whether television companies would prefer to subsidise theatrical movies and stand a chance of recouping their investment at the box office prior to transmission, as is increasingly the case with Channel 4, or whether they wouldn't rather go it alone and pass up the chance of theatrical release by concentrating on made-for-TV movies. A recent case in point is London Weekend Television's *Blue Money*, a feature-length caper comedy directed by Colin Bucksey which revealed considerable potential as a cinema movie (top British stars in an action-packed drama that covered a lot of ground in terms of landscape and locale) but which has so far had only one 'outing' – as a TV movie, arguably failing to capitalise on the greater audience who weren't watching *that night*. Naturally enough London Weekend point to the video market in refutation of the charge that such relatively expensive film-making is condemned, like some species of butterfly, to live only for one day. And indeed they may be proved right. But film-makers (writers, directors, producers, etc.) seldom feel satisfied if the energies expended 'in making movies for television all culminate in the one-off transmission, especially given the generally poor policy with regard to repeat screenings, and it is this frustration that leads many of them back to theatrical movies.

Only in some reciprocal notion of exchange between the film and television worlds whereby TV films could be allowed more chance of cinema release and cinema-based talents could be lured back into working in television can the future of a vigorous movie industry in Britain be guaranteed.

# 6

# Distributing the product

With the advent of the 'new media' – TV, cable and video – the local Odeon has become a ghost of its former self. Increasingly, producers must depend on these 'secondary' markets to turn a profit. But, as **Archie Tait** argues, these secondary markets are themselves dependent on the whole unwieldy machinery of British theatrical distributions.

Recent rumours that cinema in Britain is dead are greatly exaggerated. The fact is – though this is not shown in the existing statistics – that more people are watching more films than at any other time, including the heyday of the 1940s. By 1995 however, many of the cinemas which at present are barely able to attract audiences large enough to cover their weekly running costs will undoubtedly have closed down. Many of the smaller independent film distribution companies, sandwiched perilously between the major distributors with their multi-million dollar catalogues, and the cinema circuits which operate in their shadow, will have gone to the wall.

The key to this apparent paradox is not, of course, hard to find: television and video, the new electronic means of distributing and exhibiting films, are nudging aside the more traditional forms. Money talks. Yet, while television and video may starve cinemas of customers (and hence distributors of revenue), the newcomers cannot afford to extinguish the traditional industries completely.

There is a real sense in which the electronic media rely heavily on the existence of the old distribution/exhibition infrastructure to create the audience for the films they transmit, sell and rent, and to create the market and word-of-mouth values of those films.

This article has a single, simple thesis: that the traditional film distribution and exhibition business in Britain, and the new electronic media of broadcast and cable television and home video, are essentially interdependent, and that neither can profitably exist without the other. To the feature film industry, broadcast television represents not only a rival medium with which it competes for audience every night of the year; it also represents a supplementary or alternative means of distribution for the feature films that industry produces.

A film's television broadcast (or cable-cast or home-video distribution) is no longer supplementary to its original theatrical release in a financial sense. It is perfectly possible for producers to earn more from a television sale, or even home video sale of their films, than from the theatrical release: indeed, American companies now consider theatrical release to account for a scant 25% of a film's commercial potential. In Britain, where theatrical release is even weaker, it does not even amount to that. Both the new media are chiefly supplementary in that both the sale of the film to television, and the size of the audience it draws on transmission, are *reliant* on the scale and success of the film's original, theatrical distribution. Only when there is no hope of theatrical distribution will a producer choose to release a film directly to television or home video: this is an 'alternative' which is used only, and precisely, when there *is* no alternative.

*Television and Video*
It is the cinema infrastructure of film distribution and exhibition, with its attendant publicity machinery (including the press and media critics, and the BAFTA and Academy Awards ceremonies), which create a film's audience, and hence its value. This is value not simply to the producers and distributors, who can ask a proportionally larger sum in exchange for the television broadcast rights (as with last year's sale of *Chariots of Fire* to the BBC for a reported £1 million), but value also to the television companies, who need the large audiences a well-known film will attract to maintain their arguments for high advertising rates or licence fees.

Without having passed through the machinery of this infrastructure, *Chariots of Fire* would have had no more value than a made-for-TV movie, since it would have had no identifiable advance audience. The process of feeding a film through 'live' exhibition is still the only test which can establish that there is any desire to see a film. Unlike television programming, cinemagoing still demands that the choice be acted upon, to the extent of leaving the home or workplace and paying money to exercise the choice. And this is a demand which can be accounted.

Television has never had that demand made of it – a fact which has, in many ways, been of great benefit. While it has meant that British television programme makers have been able to get away with making and broadcasting a good deal of substandard drama, dire comedy and soporific discussion, it has also allowed television to produce dramas and current affairs programmes which would never have seen the light of day had the producers had to prove an identifiable, receptive audience for them before they went into production.

Yet minority television programming depends on the regular scheduling of other programmes which will automatically draw large audiences – ten million or more; and all that television itself has been able to come up with to do that are light entertainment (which it borrowed from the music hall tradition) and game shows. Soaps – particularly *Coronation Street* – can attract these audiences without programming support. But peak-time viewing, particularly at weekends, is often manipulated by the scheduling of feature films, in the belief that the viewers who switch on to watch the movies will then watch whatever follows.

By contrast, video and cable television distribution systems rely totally on spectators choosing to view them, and in most cases being prepared to back that choice with cash. Almost all existing existing cable services do this by programming feature films. While both video and cable have to an extent adopted the cinema's genre classification for their output (staple sex, horror, action movies), both depend utterly on distributing mass-appeal films which have a proven audience. They rely utterly, that is, on films which were originally produced for, and have been distributed through, cinemas, and have proven their drawing power in that arena.

Thus, even a cursory glance at cable television programme digests and video rental charts reveals trade dependence on films which have had successful theatrical outings.

Yet it is fair to say that, as yet, neither broadcast and cable TV nor the home video industry have even begun to recognise publicly their reliance on the theatrical film distribution and exhibition infrastructure. Gunnar Ruggheimer's parting shot when leaving his post as head of BBC Television's Programme Acquisition Department was that broadcast television not only did not owe theatrical distribution and exhibition anything, but that the film industry should be grateful to television for paying such generous prices for its product. He fiercely resisted any call for a levy on films

---

**The present tragedy of the British cinema – and you could call its whole history a series of tragedies – is that the cinema audience has largely disappeared at a point in time when the product itself is undergoing a very real revival. One can console oneself that interest in film itself here has seldom been higher. But that is not much use to an industry which still depends on an out-moded exhibition system, and which has failed so far to convince the government that it has a case for some kind of coherent encouragement. Thus the future remains as clouded and uncertain as it has always been.**

**The hope on the horizon is that film is no longer regarded by the younger generation as the least of the arts, and that its improved cultural status could eventually lead to changes in distribution and exhibition which, with effective government support, might alter the situation dramatically. If we no longer think of the cinema as *only* a mass art, but one which appeals to a whole series of interested minorities, we might one day discover an economic framework which makes much more possible.**

**Derek Malcolm, 'Guardian' Critic**

---

transmitted on television, carried on cable or distributed by video. Ruggheimer now helms the BBC's production programme for satellite and international cable distribution, so it is unlikely that he will change his view.

But it is important to recognise this view as an interested and partial one, and therefore as a pointer towards a truer picture of the situation. British television buys in its programming at absurdly low rates – rates which bear absolutely no relation either to the costs of production of the programmes, or to the initial costs of the theatrical release which gives them their high rating value. The BBC's average payment for a feature film is no more than £20,000.

And hopes that Channel 4 would improve the situation by creating competition for films were dashed with the new Channel arbitrarily setting £15,000 as its top price for a feature. And, on top of this, television usually buys films in packages, which again lowers the unit cost.

The reason for such low rates is simply historical precedent. When television first began to buy films, it was perceived by most distributors and some producers simply as extra income or a second bite at the cherry of what was essentially an ancillary market for products which had already been bought and sold on their primary (theatrical) market. It was this short-sightedness, born out of a booming industry, which is responsible for British television's refusal to take the film industry seriously on its own terms at a time when the industry has yet to recover fully from the severe slump it plunged into in the late 1960s.

Cable TV, emulating the fantastically successful model of America's Home Box Office, paid nothing towards the theatrical launch of any of the films it carried, and reaped the benefit of that launch more directly than the broadcast companies, since it carried the programming that much sooner. The small number of cable companies that so far exist in Britain – and their small audiences – has led theatrical distributors to take part in the cable trials in the same experimental frame of mind as the programming companies. But when a fuller cable system achieves greater market penetration, and with the establishment of the TEN and Premiere feature-film programming systems, there is the possibility of a new 'ghost' network, making it likely that higher and higher sums will be demanded by distributors and producers to provide the pre-sold, high-audience-rated feature-film programmes which, as with broadcast television, will be the main focus of evening programming. The reason that theatrical distributors must ask higher prices for their films is that this cinema infrastructure of theatrical distribution and exhibition is complex, unwieldly, and colossally expensive to run.

*Theatrical Distribution*

In 1983, there were 110 registered film distributors in Britain, ranging in size from United International Pictures to companies like Buzzy, Respectable and Rozier, which handle only one or two titles at any time. Of the 110 registered distributors, three large companies handle the films made by the American majors. UIP handles films from three of the 'Big Five', Paramount, Universal and MGM – plus United Artists, which MGM bought in 1982. The other two, 20th Century-Fox and Warner Brothers, are each linked with other American companies in UK distribution consortia: Fox with Walt Disney in the 1983 alliance of UK Film Distributors; and Warners with Columbia and the British company Thorn-EMI in the imaginatively titled Columbia-EMI-Warner Film Distributors. Between them, these companies handle most of the films released in British cinemas.

These companies, together with a number of smaller distributors handling British and American 'mini-major' product (Orion, which is released through Rank; Lorimar, through ITC) make up most of the membership of the Society of Film Distributors (SFD), a trade body which protects distributors' interests by operating exclusivity arrangements known as 'barring' (and recommended for outlawing by the most recent Monopolies Commission report on the British film industry), policing cinemas' accounting and return systems, sponsoring anti-piracy campaigns, and so on.

The distributors depend on widescale, low-selectivity distribution of product through the two major cinema circuits (Rank and EMI) and the smaller Cannon-Classic and Star chains. With huge print and publicity budgets to recoup, they must play their films throughout the country, and must attract a mass audience, competing with other leisure industries – music and sport, as well as broadcast and cable television and video – for their share of the nation's disposable income.

Obviously, producers must look to world markets for ultimate recoupment: Britain's cinemas represent only 3% of the world theatrical film market. Return on a single film can be significant, but the risks are high. Consider that, from the total box office take of any film, first 15% VAT is deducted, than approximately 8% had to be paid to the Eady Fund (though this is now being phased out). Of the remaining 77%, anything up to 50% will be retained by the cinema playing the film. From his remaining percentage, the distributor must cover the outlay on prints, advertising and his service overhead (usually charged as a percentage distribution fee).

On a film like *Chariots of Fire*, 20th Century-Fox recouped their initial expenses, took their distribution fee, and took their percentage share of the substantial amount of income above that level. But, bound as they were to their parent American company, they also had to lay out print and publicity costs on films like *Making*

*Love* and *Monsignor* – established flops in America which are unlikely to cover the costs of a British theatrical release.

UIP, UK (basically Fox) and C-E-W represent the major American companies. The other 101 registered film distributors are independent companies. Without the constant flow of American product which fuels the cinema chains, these companies have to fight for cinema playing time for the films they handle. Some have their own cinemas; most must bargain with circuit and independent cinema bookers for playoffs squeezed between the often extended runs of major blockbusters (and between the shorter runs of studio makeweights which are the unwritten and unspoken price for priority access to the moneyearners, in an industry where enforced blind and block booking of films is illegal).

The independent renters divide fairly obviously into those specialised in foreign and 'art-house' features, and those which attempt to play in the margins of the majors by picking up independently produced features and releasing them nationwide through the circuits. Some of the latter have leasing arrangements with American mini-major production companies, thus guaranteeing some constancy in product-flow. None the less, such tie-ups involve these smaller companies in the risk of commitment to unseen, unselected flops which may well outnumber the winners, and they must constantly look to one-off pickups of other films to defray that risk. And ultimately, the independent distributors are at the mercy of the major circuits (Rank with 76 cinemas and 197 screens, and EMI with 115 cinemas and 301 screens) and the smaller chains (Cannon-Classic with 54 cinemas and 116 screens and the Star Group with 40 cinemas and 106 screens). Without cinema outlets, the films will simply sit on the shelves.

Releasing films through the circuits is a risky business. The chains may demand that a film goes into a stipulated minimum number of their cinemas simultaneously, involving the distributor in the cost of striking ten or a dozen prints, at anything up to £1,000 each, and in buying advertising space in ten or a dozen local newspapers to promote the film. And, if the film fails to attract a large enough audience in its first, test week, it will be summarily dropped in favour of a new film or a proven warhorse from a major distributor. The risk is high; the return can be negligible. A scan of trade paper *Screen International*'s Provincial Box Office weekly listings can lead renters into instant depression: with the *top five* films each averaging between £5,000 and £1,500 per screen, the renter's share will be about 25% – anything between £1,250 and £375. Out of that, the distributor has to pay their print and publicity costs. And those are the winners!

But there is another model for independent distribution: originally pioneered by specialised London cinemas such as the Academy, the Curzon and the Paris Pullman, it is more streamlined and less risky. Instead of buying a dozen prints, the distributor makes one or two. Instead of opening at a dozen cinemas and incurring a dozen sets of house charges and break figures, a film will open at one, usually owned or leased by the distribution company. Instead of playing for one or two weeks, the film will play at least five or six, and if it is very successful, fifteen or twenty. Instead of spending between £25,000 and £40,000 to launch a film, the distributor will spend between £4,000 and £8,000. Instead of bringing back 25% of the box office, the distributor will usually bring back 50% or more in the opening weeks, slowly coming down to 25%. But, since the film will play longer, the 25%'s add up over the weeks.

Instead of taking the film to the audience through the channel of a chain of local cinemas whose running costs must be maintained, the distributor and exhibitor will, in this case, combine forces to attract the audience to the film, wherever it is playing, and undertake only a single cinema overhead. The crucial means of doing this is the local and national press, not so much through advertising, as through editorial coverage. And here, the independents have found improbable allies.

It is a matter of dismay to most of the major distributors, and to not a few successful film producers and directors, that the British film press consistently wields its influence in favour of independently produced and distributed films. It is perfectly possible to release a film successfully in Britain with one print, in one cinema, on an advertising budget of £1,000, simply on the basis of positive reviews in the key papers – *The Times, Sunday Times, Guardian, Daily* and *Sunday Telegraph, Financial Times* and *Observer*, together with London weekly listings magazines *Time Out* and *City Limits*. What counts, of course, is the perceived quality of the film in question. But there are drawbacks for the independent cinema, most notably the predominantly liberal-humanist principles which underlie the critics' perception of quality. It is a bias which influences the kind of film which an independent distributor may buy. By this token, a film by François Truffaut or Claude Goretta is likely to be snapped up for distribution, while one film by Raul Ruiz, or Helke Sander, or a Third World film-maker will have much greater difficulty in finding an opening. Of course, it must be recognised that the very respectable audiences for Tarkovsky, Bresson and recent Godard films in this country could never have been found without the support of these same 'liberal-humanist' critics. And a new film supported with sufficient conviction can still get the necessary coverage.

*Specialised Cinemas*
In London there are now 22 independent cinemas, with 27 screens. Some of them are repertory cinemas – the NFT, the Scala, the Everyman, the Barbican, the ICA Cinematheque – which specialise in rerunning classics interspersed with first runs, often in structured seasons, and in producing regular programme sheets which simultaneously explain and advertise the films they show. Most of the 22, however, are first-run cinemas attached to distribution companies: Artificial Eye's Camden Plaza, Lumiere and Chelsea; Cinegate's Gate Cinemas in Notting Hill and Bloomsbury; Mainline's Screen on the Hill, the Green, and Baker Street, together with the new Electric Screen, a former repertory cinema acquired by

Clare Higgins in *Nineteen Nineteen*

79

Mainline in 1983; Contemporary's Phoenix; and the ICA Cinema. Two of the oldest first-run cinemas, the Academy and Curzon, remain resolutely independent, serviced by a number of independent distributors, although sometimes themselves acquiring distribution rights to the films they play.

The pattern of specialised distribution outside London is slower than through the circuits, but better planned and more economical. A single print, sometimes two, will be circulated through an informal 'circuit' of independent cinemas, many of them subsidised by the British Film Institute. These cinemas usually mix first-run and repertory programming, serving the interests of their local audiences and laying an informal educational base for their localities. Like the London repertory cinemas, they produce regular programme sheets and booklets, rather than buying advertising space in local papers. They cultivate the local media, and pride themselves on building their audience through well-planned publicity and information distribution. At a time when British cinema audiences in general are falling away by percentage points each month, such cinemas have maintained theirs, and in some cases increased them.

These cinemas and their associated distribution companies have recently formed a trade association – IDEA (Independent Distributors' and Exhibitors' Association) – to represent their interests. Significantly, this organisation does not seek programming homogeneity: it is in no sense the servicing body of a new, integrated 'third circuit'. It is a body which will represent the growing number of independent cinemas which refuse alliance either with the majors or with the purely educational sector. The running costs of the 'commercial' and 'independent' film distribution and exhibition sectors clearly bear no relation to one another. Yet both are, to an increasing extent, influenced and moulded by the same factors: the increasing 'privatisation' of entertainment, the growing dominance of home-based, rather than extra-mural recreation.

The extreme positions in both commercial and independent sectors are squeezed least. On the one hand, the large American-based entertainment companies, themselves now only subdivisions of larger, diversified multinational corporations with a large stake in cable and satellite television and in video distribution and manufacture, will continue to make their high-cost, high-risk productions. Protected on one side by their ability to produce annual portfolios of films which spread the risk across a number of productions, and on the other side by their ability to sell the whole package through all the distribution media, taking profit at each stage, they will not only survive: they will go on being immensely profitable. On the other hand, the independent distributor-exhibitors will continue to flourish, supported by a loyal and informed audience and by a well-developed critical and media apparatus. By pegging costs, and through an increasing ability to sell product on the video and television distribution channels, they will produce small but steady profits.

But most if not all of the intervening spectrum of distribution and, particularly, exhibition is bound to collapse. Major conurbations will continue to support one or two cinemas, as they continue to support one or two theatres. In those cities, the circuit cinemas, playing major productions, will coexist with independent, subsidised, education-linked theatres. Outside those cities, public cinema, like public theatre, will cease to exist – other, perhaps, than as another form of 'arts touring'. The reasons for this pared-down theatrical infrastructure are partly to do with a continued demand for cinema as a participatory, social, audience-involved phenomenon, but mainly to do with servicing the other, electronic media which will undoubtedly increase their financial and social dominance. The electronic media will continue to need the theatrical infrastructure as pre-publicity, and also to a lesser extent as a research and development project – a testing ground for the audience reaction substantially denied these media by the necessarily private nature of the operation.

Beyond these temperate predictions lies the whole question of the kind of trade legislation which will encourage, or at least allow, them. As things now stand, the film industry on the one hand, and broadcast and cable on the other, came under different government departments, while film culture comes under a third. The film industry comes under the Department of Trade, film culture under the Office of Arts and Libraries, and broadcasting under the Home Office. This separation has grown up and been maintained for perfectly understandable reasons. The film industry, with a small home market, needs the support of a department geared towards foreign exchange and trade. Film education and culture to a certain extent need the protection from the vagaries of the international market place which inclusion in the 'Arts' sector allows. Television, as the principal communicator and as a powerful force in the formation and even inculcation of ideas of the way we exist and develop as a nation, needs to be seen in the context of other national democratic institutions.

That separation, however, has led to blockages in the interaction of film and television industries. And it is on this separation that legislative rationalisation has foundered. Whether this kind of legislation can be fought through remains open to doubt. But there can be *no* doubt that it would create a healthier, more equable climate for promoting the undoubted skill and talent that British film and television have already developed, and for encouraging the kind of independent audio-visual industry and culture which is the corollary of the changes in film viewing and entertainment needs which the new media have brought.

# 7

# Declarations of independence

Until very recently, an independent British cinema,
motivated more by politics than commerce, was either a
distant memory or a far-off dream.
**Sheila Whitaker** charts the progress of the independent
cinema movement through the 1970s to the present,
placing in context the work of regional film-making groups
now seeking outlets on television, and poses
urgent questions about the future of low-budget,
'grassroots' film-making in Britain.

Independent film-making in Britain has a relatively short history
and its current identification as a 'movement' can be held to date
from the formation in 1974 of the IFA, the Independent Film-
makers' Association. There had, of course, been independent film
activity earlier in the century. The introduction of 16mm film stock
in the 1930s liberated film from the commercial system and enabled
'independent' films to be screened in venues other than cinemas
and to avoid censorship, chiefly of a political nature.

As a result of this development, 'independence' came to be
understood as a political or ideological stance within film-making:
in exhibition through the work of, for example, Kino and the
Progressive Film Institute (PFI); and in production through the
work of the Socialist Films Council, the Workers' Film and Photo
League and the PFI, as well as the films of Ivor Montagu, Ralph
Bond and Sidney Cole.

These films had their origins in the activity of the Communist
Party of Great Britain and a good many were concerned with the

international anti-fascist struggles of the 1930s rather than with narrower nationally focused issues such as class. They dealt not only with Spain but with other areas of fascist advance such as in Abyssinia and Czechoslovakia.

The next blossoming of independent film-making was in the 1950s with Karel Reisz and Lindsay Anderson spearheading the 'Free Cinema' movement. Now frequently and perhaps unfairly dismissed as a retrograde step for British independent cinema, Free Cinema was specifically singled out by the IFA in 1976 for being:

> anti-theoretical and unable to articulate any class position... concerned with conventional notions of the artist reworked in terms of a liberal humanist commitment. ... The entire concept of independence during this period was elaborated within the basic cultural framework established by the industry.[1]

Free Cinema's undeniable positive achievement was that it briefly held out the possibility of a different cinema in Britain. Anderson, Reisz and Richardson all went on to make feature films, which initially at least could be seen as part of a 'new wave' of commercial film-making. But it never posed the question of a cinema that would remain different – whether in cultural or organisational terms.

The 'Underground' film movement of the 1960s in America formed part of a wider move to erect an alternative culture. It was short on political and ideological analysis but was remarkably successful in confronting issues and mobilising protest. As its influence spread throughout the Western world, a variety of new independent film-making groups emerged, the most significant of which, for Britain, was the London Film-makers' Co-op. Initially a union of film-makers working as individuals in film aesthetics as well as political production, it organised screenings and then in 1970 was able to make production equipment available.

Meanwhile, in the latter half of the 1960s, cultural and political changes in Britain led, among other things, to a renewed concern with questions of representation and reporting and with the institutional control of the media. It was widely felt to be important both to produce alternative representations and reports and to distribute them independently. The Angry Arts Group (to become Liberation Films in 1970) began work around the exhibition process itself as well as producing their own films. In 1968, the earliest and one of the most important film workshops, Cinema Action, took this a stage further by touring the country and screening films (including their own) in places such as factories, pubs and Trade Union premises. These early collectives were followed by Amber Films in Newcastle in 1969, Berwick Street Film Collective in 1970, the London Women's Film Group in 1972, Four Corners Films in 1973 and The Other Cinema as a distribution agency in 1970.

Independent film-making, however, needs funding since film-makers, however committed, cannot indefinitely survive, let alone be effective, without it. The irony is, of course, that funding to any substantial degree has to come from central or local government sources (commercial sponsorship, discounting the case of Channel 4, is not a real factor in present circumstances), and often this state funding can, as a result, be required for work which is explicitly opposed to state ideologies as presently constituted. Nevertheless the Arts Council in 1972 established a fund for individual films, with the proviso that these were to be involved in questions of fine art and aesthetics and not in broader political matters, and gradually Regional Arts Associations, beginning with Northern Arts in 1968, began small-scale funding of individuals.

The British Film Institute, however, which was the main potential source of finance for the sector, was significantly either unwilling or very slow to recognise its responsibilities in the area. Its reluctance to act became even more apparent with its refusal to provide any grant aid for The Other Cinema, the independent distributor which opened a cinema in 1976 in central London which very quickly ran into financial difficulties. Instead the BFI continued to expand and support its hotch-potch of Regional Film Theatres, some of which operated only one day a week and which were all, almost without exception, firmly embedded in the art-house tradition of exhibition.

In 1974 the Independent Film-makers' Association was established, aiming to provide a properly constituted organisation which could effectively promote the interests of independent film-makers and mobilise such forces as were vital to create viable structures for independent production. Inevitably there were problems: film-makers' interests could potentially be as many and various as there were film-makers. Essentially, though, the divergences were two: firstly, between those who wished to work within the mainstream and those who wished to work outside it in the hope of transforming not only cinema itself but also the social and cultural context; and secondly between those who wished to engage in directly political activity in production and exhibition (which included raising questions about the values implicit in realism and documentary) and those who wished to involve themselves principally in specifically aesthetic issues in terms of film as film. Problems of policy and practice were heavily underscored by other problems of organisation and administration – not least that there was no funding for an organiser of an organisation whose members were scattered throughout the country and involved in their own projects as well as, often, other work that paid the rent. Nevertheless the IFA succeeded in putting pressure on the BFI, resulting in the right to nominate two members to the BFI Production Board and then, in 1980, obtaining grant aid for the IFA itself.

As part of its activities, the IFA also attempted to dominate the BFI Annual Conference in the late 1970s and early 80s. These conferences had started as a forum for independent regional exhibitors, but with the advent of a recognisable independent production sector the presence and arguments of the producers had been welcomed by most, if not all, exhibitors. The IFA's intervention can now be seen as having two major outcomes. On the positive side, it quite properly brought to the forefront of exhibitors' minds (many of whom, it has to be said, were still very much tied to the art-house tradition) the importance of supporting indigenous independent film-making and contributing towards its assured future by exhibiting independent films. Less productively, however, the independent film-makers' lobby took to using the conference to pursue sectional ends in opposition to those of the other groups represented there. Regretfully the exhibitors came to the conclusion that a forum for mutual dialogue, for the sake of which the conference had been opened out to include production, had become the object of counter-productive lobbying by an organisation whose members were devoted to promoting their own interests with little sense of where or how their films were going to be shown outside the few existing workshops. Undoubtedly there were, and still are, many independent producers who understood the importance of obtaining wider exhibition and the problems for the exhibitors in securing it for them. But the overwhelming sense that exhibitors had, rightly or wrongly, of independent producers totally absorbed in their own worlds came to a head at the 1982 Conference, as a result of which the exhibitors and distributors set up their own organisation, the Independent Exhibitors and Distributors Association (IDEA).[2]

Meanwhile, the idea of the film workshop was gaining ground. New workshops came into being – Sheffield Film Co-op (a feminist group), Birmingham Film Workshop, Chapter in Cardiff, and a second Tyneside workshop, Trade Films. Then, in 1982, the ACTT, in association with the BFI and Channel 4, instituted the 'Grant-Aided Workshops Production Declaration', by which independent workshops could be franchised under union agreements. This had been preceded by an ACTT 'Code of Practice' which had been prompted by the disparity between the funding available for BFI Production Board films and those funded by Regional Arts Associations. The Code was to be implemented by agreement with the larger RAAS, but its voluntary aspect highlighted the anomalies in independent production. Support began to build up for the ACTT's campaign against low wages and casualisation (in the independent sector often no wages) and the union set up a Committee for Independent Grant-Aided Film which culminated in the Workshops Declaration. This funding initiative was aimed specifically at 'workshops and other organisations eligible for accreditation under this Declaration which shall be exclusively those whose sources of revenue funding are derived from public bodies, charities and other organisations and individuals, where it is explicitly stated and understood that funding is provided on a totally non-commercial and non-profit distributing basis'; and it was drawn up 'in the explicit belief and with the explicit intention of encouraging the cultural, social and political contribution made to society by the grant-aided and non-commercial production activities historically undertaken by persons and organisations in this sector.' Substantially it ensured the rights of members of workshops not only to basic employment rights, including a minimum annual salary of £8,000 (a minimum which very few personnel involved in regional independent exhibition attain), but it also stated that 'all rights in productions originated by the permanently employed staffs within a Workshop or other organisation recognised under this Declaration shall be held collectively by those staffs and all contractual arrangements shall be approved collectively by the staffs employed under the terms of this Declaration within any Workshop or other organisation', and established an agreed quota of films produced by such workshops which could be screened by Channel 4.

The Workshops Declaration was a fundamental step forward for independent productions and the people involved, but inevitably some had (and still have) doubts about the long-term impact of

*Workers' Playtime* (Channel 4)

union involvement. The ACTT is a highly structured organisation, geared to protectionism within a media industry whose film section is diminishing in importance. Independent film-makers may be forgiven for sometimes wondering to what extent the ideological and cultural implications of the Declaration have permeated the union as a whole. Added to this is the concern that the justifiable demand for secure employment within independent production may channel energy into 'trade-union' issues rather than into film-making itself. There is an increasing recognition that, in the present climate, the chances of new workshops emerging such as Cinema Action and Amber who survived and progressed for years on the energies and commitment of their members is increasingly unlikely. For every film made in Britain through the unpaid toil and commitment of its makers, there are undoubtedly hundreds in other countries, in North America and Western Europe as much as in the Third World. Indeed American film-makers alongside their Third World counterparts do seem to consider their films as more important than anything else. Jon Jost and Les Blank are prime examples of the ability for self-help, as are film-makers such as Anand Patwardhan and Aribam Syam Sharma from India.

An essential part of the Workshops development was the establishment of Channel 4, which, even before it began broadcasting in November 1982, had expressed a commitment to alternative and independent film-making. With the start of Channel 4 independent film-makers could at last see the possibility of a major outlet for their films. The rush to submit proposals was almost embarrassing to onlookers, and not a little ironic to those exhibitors who had struggled to produce audiences for independent film-making. Suddenly film-makers seemed not unreasonably delirious on the heady notion of a constant market, an audience comprising hundreds of thousands rather than tens.

Sadly, however, much of the material produced at the end of the 1970s and early 80s and transmitted in the early months of Channel 4 was seen starkly for what it was: material inaccessible to the larger audience. Even with the best will in the world, television audiences found it hard to come to terms with films originally designed for an audience of cognoscenti. Thus the problem with which independent exhibitors had struggled – how to build audiences for films which, by their nature, assume a fairly high level of knowledge of and concern with the issues of film aesthetics, not least those of realism and of social and cultural politics – was brutally and embarrassingly foregrounded.

In 1978 Sylvia Harvey had written an important monograph which accurately (and in some case prophetically) raised a number of these issues.[3] She began:

> Given the present system of social relations and of relations in the cinema, only the very wealthy are 'independent'. Without the private means not only to finance a film project but beyond that to buy up a few cinemas in which to show the film, or at the very least a few projectors with which to show it, no film-maker is 'independent'. Rather, what we need to understand and analyse are the complex series of dependencies which characterise the position of the non-commercial film-maker. What must be emphasised is the fact of dependence on whatever system of finance presents itself. 'Independents' are part of an economic system which contains and to some extent controls their production. The important question then becomes, from within that dependency, what are the possible areas of action, the possible areas of freedom within the larger constraints?

She goes on to point out that freedom from the constraints of box-office returns, the 'more ferocious currents of commercial interests', can itself be a dubious privilege since 'the same operation which isolates the film-maker from commercial constraints and from the mainstream of market relations, also isolates the film-makers from a range of consumers, that is from a range of possible audiences.' The alternative to this isolation, derived from the dominant cinema's refusal to exhibit such films, is the notion of what she calls an 'oppositional space'. But, she observes:

> To oppose mainstream cinema, it is not enough to produce a cinema which is in opposition to the mainstream at the level of the mode of production, the counter cinema must also be in opposition to the mainstream at the level of 'consumption'; by this I mean that any genuinely 'counter' cinema must engage in the battle for audiences. Moreover what needs to be constructed is not an 'alternative' culture – a safe place – the eternal safe place of the avant garde, but an oppositional culture which engages with dominant forms not only at the level of form and content, but also in terms of an analysis of those existing social processes within which culture production is inserted.

She concludes:

> Any avant garde which fails to engage with the question of who are the consumers, who are the spectators, and beyond that with questions about the nature of the social system which determines the fact of there being certain spectators, and certain patterns of consumption, is doomed to occupy an alternative and not an oppositional space in relationship to mainstream cinema. Such an isolated and ignorant avant garde can only contribute to the reproduction of existing social relations and not to their trans-formation.

This takes us back to the point which I made in my discussion of the relationships between independent film-makers and exhibitors as evidenced at the Regional Conferences – namely that the former seemed to have entirely forgotten for whom the films were made, where they were to be shown outside their own 'oppositional' spaces, and therefore why their films should be considered import-ant enough to be funded in the first place and supported by distributors and exhibitors after completion. The muddled thinking apparent in the late 1970s was compounded by the advent of Channel 4. The indecent rush of indepedent film-makers to have their films screened on the new channel only highlighted this inability or unwillingness to consider questions of audience, questions (it might be observed) vitally informed by issues of ideology and cultural and social history of the very type which many film-makers were addressing in the content of their films. Although the independent 'slot' in Channel 4 was always late at night, thus forcing it into a ghetto even in the age of time-slip recording, the question still needs to be asked: could many of these films have been screened earlier and proved capable not only of achieving reasonable viewing figures but, most importantly, operating in such a way to engage with audiences.

Channel 4 now finds itself under pressure to attain higher audience figures and to be less 'left-wing', both of which factors militate against any substantial programming of independent film work. It is in relation to the needs of the larger audiences, whether those of regional cinemas or of Channel 4, that I would part company with some of Sylvia Harvey's comments in a later paper presented at the 1980 BFI Regional Conference.[4] The IFA, she says:

> has been to the forefront in developing these arguments about the cultural importance of cinema. What I would like to argue is that because independent film-makers are involved in production for cultural, artistic or social reasons and not for commercial reasons they are able to take much more seriously the needs of their audiences. They are able to think about the relationship between their activity in production and the audience's activity in consumption, and to think about the ways in which the audience is already (and in relation to a wide variety of types of film) involved in quite an active way in watching and 'reading' film and that it therefore already takes part in producing the meaning of that film.

The disagreement is not so much over the IFA's arguments as over the practice, since this concept of a cinema of social practice has not, by and large, taken account of the audiences for film that have been produced by regional cinemas where a transformation of cinema viewing is already taking place. More needs to be done to increase the adaptability of existing exhibition spaces, to free them from the 'hot-house' of art cinema and move them, albeit gradually, into the area of genuine social practice where issues around the production of meaning can be raised. With mutual co-operation this can be achieved. On the one hand it entails the recognition by exhibitors of a progressive exhibition policy – that is to say, one

which regards exhibition as the beginning of their work, not the end
– but on the other hand film-makers must also recognise not just
the necessity but their duty to make films which are accessible and
can be used by exhibitors with their audiences.

As one way of engaging with the audiences' role in film,
independent film-makers, more often than not, wish to travel with
their films – a desire arising out of the recognition of the relationship between production and consumption as described by
Sylvia Harvey. However this practice itself raises issues. Firstly, to
what extent do they feel the need to direct, inform or explain their
films, in other words to intervene between their film and the
audience in a way which might either suggest an attempt directly to
influence or even to foreclose the production of meaning from
outside the film in a manner no less arbitrary than the operation of
mainstream cinema? Secondly, is this practice complicit in the
notion of authorship (albeit collective authorship) – an ideology
which, to a great extent, independent film-makers regard as
bourgeois, anti-theoretical and unprogressive? This is not to say
that such activity should not go on, but rather that there may be a
danger that film-makers are less concerned with their films as part
of an overall oppositional practice in which the interest and needs

*The Gold Diggers*

92

of the audience are paramount than with apparently wishing to ensure the status of their single text, understandable though this is. To what extent do they really understand and accept that their films *are but single elements in an on-going practice dedicated to key issues and debates,* and can therefore be used in a variety of ways and in a variety of contexts, each of which will itself transform the meaning production of an individual film? It is this *flexibility* of use which precisely ensures the possibility of subverting the notion of a consumerist cinema.

A major failing of contemporary British independent cinema has been its almost wilful refusal to engage with narrative forms. To some extent this derives from what was felt to be a prior need to engage with the residues of the British documentary tradition and not just to criticise that tradition theoretically but to produce films which addressed contemporary problems and reinterpreted past and present struggles (particularly over class and women's issues), with new forms as well as new contents. The work of Frank Abbott and of the Berwick Street Collective is particularly interesting in this respect. However, this concentration on areas where documentary forms can be used and simultaneously deconstructed has had two negative effects. On the one hand it has led to the neglect of certain issues (such as nuclear power/nuclear weapons) where a more straightforward approach might be appropriate. On the other hand, and even more importantly, it has given further impetus to the flight from narrative. An almost obsessive wish to sever once and for all the desire of audiences for the pleasures of seamless fiction (as if this were even possible) has severely hampered the independent movement's ability to handle narrative forms in any way at all. Richard Woolley (*Telling Tales, Brothers and Sisters*) and, latterly, Sally Potter (*The Gold Diggers*) and Bette Gordon (*Variety*) are perhaps the only examples of film-makers from the independent movement who have been able to combine critical and reflexive concerns with the construction of pleasurable narratives. Whatever one's attitude to the ideology of narrative, one ignores at one's peril the fundamental role that narrative has always played in Western society (indeed in any society). The real challenge, therefore, lies not in hoping that the desire for narrative will simply go away or in trying to persuade audiences that they should resist it, but in finding ways of intelligently recreating narrative forms, operating perhaps under a different 'regime of pleasure production', but pleasurable none the less.

The narrative film which is not a theatrical feature is, however, one of the hardest forms for which to find audiences and distribution. A lot depends on the initiative of distributors and exhibitors in finding modes of release and programming for films which bridge the entrenched divide between the commercial entertainment feature and the political or instructional short. Although throughout the 1970s independent distribution and exhibition has not been as progressive and active as many film-makers might have wished, attempts have been made to come to grips with the necessity of foregrounding independent work and re-producing contemporary audiences for it. The Other Cinema, for all its problems, not least of administration and effectivity (partly but not wholly caused by lack of finance), has been a major source of independent distribution both British and international of a directly political body of work – films, that is, which 'seek to change people's perceptions of political, social or personal situations'. The Other Cinema distributes to regional cinemas, film societies, political groups, etc. and it is true to say that without its activity there would not have been any truly independent distribution to speak of for most of the 1970s. Alongside The Other Cinema there are now two specialised feminist distribution groups, Cinema of Women and Circles. Established in 1980, cow films have, from small beginnings, built up a noteworthy catalogue of material largely distributed to womens' groups, schools, etc. But in the last three or four years they have adventurously attempted to bring feminist cinema into a wider political consciousness. This began with the revival of *Mädchen in Uniform* exhibited at the Screen on the Green in 1981. Their first contemporary big-screen launch was with *A Question of Silence* in 1982, followed by *Born in Flames* in 1983. cow are now the major feminist distributors in Britain, but it is difficult for them to survive without grant aid. In a smaller way, Circles has also built up a solid policy towards individual films (including some from the 'avant garde'), and in addition to their normal distribution have established a creative exhibition relationship with the Four Corners Workshop in East London.

The exhibition sector is currently in a state of flux. In the later 1960s and early 70s when the BFI's grand-aided sector (the so-called 'Regional Film Theatres') was built up, programming policy was muddled and counter-productive, owing to a situation where local lay people, for example local councillors who held one set of pursestrings, sat on programme committees, and were

94

'advised' by professionals from London who held the other set. In this situation – aggravated, it must be said, by the near impossibility of doing anything remotely sensible with one screening a week – programming was backward, unexciting and ill informed. The response from the BFI was to propose, and to some extent impose, centralised programming by the 'experts' in London, despite all the evidence against its fruitfulness both from within the better regional cinemas and, of course, from the experience of the commercial circuits where regional initiative, expertise and variation were completely stamped out by Wardour Street to everyone's cost.

The alternative which began to be prospected in the mid-1970s was to concentrate investment on a few two-screen cinemas in major urban centres such as Manchester, Birmingham, Bristol and Newcastle and at the same time establish other smaller (but still full-time) cinemas in other cities, all with their own professional staff and adequate financial resources. A decade later, this policy is coming to fruition with the BFI's support of the multi-technology venues established at Bristol's Watershed, at the Greater Manchester Arts Centre and at Tyneside Cinema in Newcastle where a brand-new multi-technology centre is under construction. These centres also have, or will have, library and reference resources, bookshops, video libraries, etc. for general use.

Meanwhile, over the last five years many exhibitors in the grant-aided sector have recognised the importance of a more progressive exhibition policy, one which engages in *issues* rather than just in the mechanics of presenting isolated new releases or one-off films for general consumption. This policy includes work with local and special-interest groups and implicitly recognises film not simply as entertainment after the day is done but as a cogent and integral element in the social, cultural and political context of people's lives. A progressive exhibition policy of this kind is fundamental to the new independent cinema in that it enables ideas and connections to be made not simply between one film and another but between film and the social and political context. The real strength of these regional cinemas lies in their grass-roots support and the energy and professionalism of their staff and their ability to carve out their own futures.

One of the ways in which independent productions can acquire more visibility is in a festival context, but even this is beset with problems. Festivals do generate publicity, both locally and nationally, and independent film can benefit from this. But it is still in danger of getting lost beneath the other concerns both of the festival itself and of the media. Mainstream productions will always get most of the limelight. Media attention is almost exclusively focused on 'releases', and independent films do not get released. Equally damaging to any attempts to put independent film-making on the map is the deeply ingrained notion that anything that

---

**Being a film producer in England in 1985 is bewildering. Continuous requests from journalists across Europe for interviews suggest that they know something you don't. But in fact they are all merely chasing each other's hype about the new British cinema. Their view of someone producing films in London as someone at the centre of a dynamic surge of creative energy is far indeed from the actual experience; an experience of scarcity, deviousness and stark pessimism.**

**During the press conference after a screening of the recent BFI release, *Nineteen Nineteen*, at the Berlin Film Festival this year, I was asked what structures existed to allow the making of films to such professional standards yet without obvious commercial intent. The answer was a description of a system that soon will have no provision for the art of cinema to the extent that this differs from the commerce of cinema; of a country in which people whose work would be valued by industry and government in any other European country often left unable to work at all; and of the most backward official attitude to independent cinema anywhere in Europe.**

**Peter Sainsbury, Producer**

---

happens in the London is national but anything that happens in regions is 'provincial'. This attitude, combined with the lack of an integrated national network of production, distribution and exhibition, has hampered the construction of, at the very least, a genuinely plural national film culture. Nevertheless festival screenings potentially can be a major avenue for the creation of audiences for independent film so long as certain basic practices are implicit in the festival structure. Firstly, independent film must be presented in its own right and not as an adjunct – the poor, but sometimes bright, country cousin of mainstream production. Secondly, to the extent funds permit, the screening of the films should be accompanied by other events such as seminars, workshops and discussions, and by publications, dealing with the issues raised both in and by the films in the programme.

The Edinburgh Film Festival in the 1970s, under the direction of Lynda Myles, did a tremendous amount of work with independent film-makers and with films on the fringes of the mainstream industry. Much of the work promoted was American and had higher budgets and less directly political objectives than the work of many British film-makers today. Nevertheless the festival was quite subversive of mainstream practices and did a lot to generate interest in work outside the mainstream. The Tyneside Film Festival has, since 1980, carried on some of this work, but with a different emphasis. It has aimed to provide a forum for contemporary independent film-makers and give a profile to the sector which would enable regional audiences to engage with it. Work both from Britain and from abroad has been screened. The aim has been not only to bring in larger audiences, drawn from a wider spread of the population, than one would normally expect for such films, but to get the audience to engage with the films with different expectations than they would bring to more mainstream productions.

The Tyneside Film Festival has also always been international. This has meant that film-makers and audiences alike have the benefit of being able to compare films of different nationalities and different production contexts. In 1983 the Festival screened over 130 international productions of all lengths and types, including (for the first time that year) a substantial amount of video. Since the Festival is devoted solely to independent cinema, it has been possible for it to engage with the notions of politics, ideology, meaning production and exhibition practice which are urgent concerns of the independent sector in Britain, and to situate all these questions in an international perspective.

In 1982, the Festival became competitive, with the creation of the £5,000 Tyne Award (funded by Newcastle City Council) given to the film-maker whose film screened in the Festival best indicated the potential of independent film-making. The Award that year was won by Anand Patwardhan, a film-maker from Bombay, for his films *A Time to Rise* and *Prisoners of Conscience*. In 1983 it was won by Chris Reeves for *The Cause of Ireland*, and three other smaller awards were instituted – a Short Film Award (which went to Jacki McKimmie of Australia for *Stations*), an Award for the best film from the North East (Tony Harrild for *Homeground*) and the Tyne Video Limited Award for the best video (Skip Sweeney for

97

*My Father Sold Studebakers*). 1984 saw the establishment of the Sandra Russell Award for the best individual contribution by a female or third-world person to any film screened in the Festival. These are all important and progressive steps since, aside from providing funds for independent film-makers, the Awards also had the advantage of providing greater media coverage for the Festival and therefore for the sector as such. However it does not alter the fundamental necessity for the Festival to organise its programme in such a way that the films contribute to the overall project of (re)producing audiences.

Independent film-making in Britain is very much at a watershed. Just as everything, in 1982-83, seemed to be set fair, cracks have appeared both in the role Channel 4 has (or is able) to play and within the IFA (now IFVA) itself. Success (relative though it still is) has, perhaps, prompted the emergence of the conflicting interests which were always to be found beneath the surface of IFA unity or indeed to be found in the initial opposition between those who wanted the opportunity to be independent whilst distributed and exhibited in the mainstream and those who wanted to transform it. The result is that the strength evidenced in the late 1970s and early 80s has to a great extent evaporated. A lot now depends on the initiative of individual film-makers in creating forms of work which can find a place within the available exhibition structures, whether as film, video or TV. But even more depends on the evolution of the structures themselves, which dictate the possibilities available to film-makers. A dynamic of independence has been built up over the past decade which is not going to be dissipated and real inroads can be made into the space created by the dwindling of the dominant cinema. Perhaps, however the most important element will be, as it always has been, the will and ability of all concerned to disregard sectarian interests and co-operate in developing independent cinema, in all its forms, as the vital force in cultural life that it undoubtedly has the potential to be.

# 8

# Charioteers
# and Ploughmen

The 'Britishness' of British cinema has always
been a vexed question. It is raised in particularly acute
form by two key films of the 1980s – the proud,
exportable *Chariots of Fire* and the far less triumphal
*The Ploughman's Lunch.*
**Sheila Johnston** examines the two films in detail,
contrasting the views they offer of what it means to be British
and looking at how this is represented in film.

When *Chariots of Fire*, not exactly a front runner in the Oscar
stakes, romped home on 23 March 1982 with the prize for
Best Picture and three further Academy Awards to boot, its status
was secured as the emissary and emblem of what pundits were later
pleased to call the 'British film renaissance'. That status was confirmed rather than challenged by *Gandhi*'s grand slam of eight
Oscars the following year. And other subsequent critical and/or
commerical successes – *Educating Rita, Another Country, Grey-
stoke, Local Hero* – merely served to vindicate the proud, patriotic
claim that 'the British are coming!' made by *Chariots* writer Colin
Welland at the Oscar ceremony and promulgated the next morning
via half-page advertisements taken by the production company
Goldcrest in the national press.

The euphoria was, inevitably, attended by sour reminders that
this quintessentially British film had been entirely financed by
foreign backers, as well as cynical speculation about the politics
behind the prizes. The British trade press, for instance, remarked

that *Chariots* had been cited in *American Film* as one of President Reagan's two favourite movies of 1981 (the other being the Australian *Breaker Morant*); that its major rival for the Best Picture Award was the ideologically untimely *Reds*; and that the senior membership of the Academy had a distinct right-of-centre tinge. Rather than being a simple case of the best film having won, it was implied, *Chariots* had been lauded as a vehicle for the stirring sentiments of the New Conservatism.[1]

Director Hugh Hudson did not see it entirely like that:

> Villains? The bigoted establishment? In a sense that is the dichotomy of the film. In a way it is pro-traditionalist and could be accused of being very conservative. And yet you have the two main characters fighting against various kinds of bigotry.[2]

Indeed, these conflicts are worked through in *Chariots* with a sophistication which gives the lie to critics who saw it as another 'retro' period piece or a simple-mindedly ripping yarn. Harold Abrahams (Ben Cross), a Jew of Lithuanian extraction, and Eric Liddell (Ian Charleson), a Scottish missionary, both students at Cambridge and keen runners, try for selection for the 1924 Paris Olympics team. Despite racial prejudice and disapproval of his ruthless professionalism, Abrahams runs and wins a gold medal in the prestigious 100 metres race. Liddell, a devout Sabbatarian, firmly refuses to take part in his heat, scheduled for a Sunday, despite cajoling from the Prince of Wales (David Yelland). But in the end a colleague, Lord Lindsey (Nigel Havers), stands down, enabling Liddell to replace him in his own event – the 400 metres – where Liddell also wins his gold and sets a world record.

In this way Liddell's enforced choice between God and King is avoided rather than resolved, and his national identity as a Scot, apart from a couple of early scenes set in Scotland, where there is much bagpipe playing and swirling of kilts, is never much at issue. It is around the figure of Abrahams, the foreigner who aspires to become a true Englishman, that the narrative is organised (the film opens and ends with his funeral) and that these questions most sharply cohere. Abrahams' naked ambition quickly incurs the displeasure of the doyens of the Establishment, the Masters of Trinity and Caius Colleges (John Gielgud and Lindsay Anderson) who, in key confrontation, berate him for hiring the Italian-Arab Sam Massabini (Ian Holm) as his coach. The problem is that Massabini – and Abrahams – are not only aliens, but also grubby professionals,

impudent parvenus. The questions of nationality and class are collapsed together: Englishness is identified by them with the inherited privilege of Cambridge's *jeunesse dorée*.

The chief representative of all this is Lindsey – born, as Welland's screenplay neatly puts it, with a whole canteen of silver cutlery in his mouth. He is the gentleman sportsman whose typically idiosyncratic training method – jumping hurdles balanced with glasses that are brimming with champagne – offsets Massabini's more punishing and 'serious' programme. Charming, sybaritic, verging on the dissolute, Lindsey is none the less aware that changes are afoot, that aristocracy must cede to the new meritocracy, and he gallantly stands down for his chums (Abrahams in love, Liddell in his race) in a true act of *noblesse oblige*.

Thus nationality, and the social status that accompanies it, are honours that can be *earned*, not just acquired by inheritance. Abrahams 'becomes' an Englishman by virtur of his Olympic victory: symbolically, Massabini, waiting anxiously back at the hotel, learns of this by seeing the Union Jack hoisted aloft and hearing 'God Save the King' played in the distance. On their triumphant return, he and the rest of the team are greeted with newspaper headlines (now heavy with post-Falklands resonance) that declare:

'Our boys are home.' Returning, full cycle, to his funeral, we even find Abrahams described at his death as 'the Elder Statesman of British Athletics', as we hear that wonderfully traditional sound of the voices of choristers lifted in song. And what are they singing but the grand old Blakean hymn which lends the film its title and which, in calling for Jerusalem to be built in England's green and pleasant land, aptly stands for the synthesis of Abrahams' twin origins?

David Puttnam, the film's producer, has identified two apparently incompatible interpretations of *Chariots*:

> Don Boyd tells me that *Chariots of Fire* is a jingistic picture. I don't think it is. I think it's a film about the victory of the individual over the state. He honestly believes it's a film about the state's domination of the individual.[3]

Both sides are right. Abrahams is the 'foreign body' who irritates the Establishment, but who is eventually assimilated, thereby changing it: individual and state are, accordingly to the rhetoric of *Chariots*, a fake opposition. The opening sequence, as conceived in Welland's second draft screenplay, makes this abundantly clear (perhaps *too* clear, since it has been lost from the final film):

> Filling screen – BIG CLOSE UP – a medal, a gold medal hanging on a 'sky blue' East German chest. The GDR dirge ploughs on above the image. Then PULL BACK to see the recipient, erect, bland, smiling a practised smile, programmed. Back further to encompass his team mates, second and third, cast from the same mould. They stand – a triumphant, manufactured trio. Back again to reveal they are images on a screen, a TV screen. Back further – more screens, the image multiplied a score or more.

And thence to the funeral service. At the end, we were to return to the TVs to discover a despondent loser and Lindsey, emerging from the church, was to remark jocularly that 'all that fellow needs [is] a week at Broadstairs', *Chariots* indicates, then, that the state's 'domination of the individual' need not reign supreme (it is, of course, no coincidence that the TV trio are Communist clones: remember that the script was written in the shadow of the 1980 Moscow Olympics), thus fulfilling Hudson's claim for it as at once iconoclastic *and* deeply conservative.

Interestingly, and despite his above disclaimer, Puttnam's carefully supervised publicity campaign has presented *Chariots*, in Britain at least, very much in terms of a nostalgic and rather innocent *Boy's Own* patriotism, in the studied artlessness of both the original 'biscuit tin' poster design and the cinema trailer. The latter begins with a caption and voice-over announcing that 'it's easy to forget how wonderful British films used to be', duly followed by a series of memory-jogging clips displaying those films in all their infinite variety, from thriller to melodrama to musical to epic: *The Third Man, Brief Encounter, Oliver, Lawrence of Arabia, Henry V*... But, as Sir Larry delivers his Agincourt address ('We few, we happy few, we band of brothers...'), the image slowly shrinks and the sound fades away, drowned out by the narrator's voice. 'Nowadays, the only place you see British films like these is on television. What happened?' wonders the voice. 'America, that's

---

**What we have in Britain is essentially a suburban cinema – safe, cosy, anonymous and built between the two wars. What we need is a cinema like the heart of a city – exciting and dangerous in equal measures.**

**Michael Radford, Director**

---

what happened. Suddenly every film takes place in Los Angeles, New York, San Francisco. Which is why Twentieth Century-Fox are so very proud...' Cue to the celebrated Broadstairs beach scene that was to become so well-known that Michael Palin could raise a laugh by 'quoting' it in *The Missionary* and that a TV shoe ad that showed children running along the sand to the strains of Vangelis sound-alike music could be banned for plagiarism. The message is spelled out one last time – 'In this age of the all-American movie, a British film about British heroes' – and the trailer ends.

It seems almost preposterously naive, but in-depth historical analysis is scarcely to be expected from a three-minute trailer, and anyway our narrator patently has his tongue at least half-way in his cheek. There's a knowingness in this little trailer, and of course *a fortiori* in the film itself, that makes *Chariots* more than just the acceptable face of that other form of disguised patriotism, the Bond movie, where jingoism is often cynically reduced, as in London Weekend Television's tribute[4] to 'doing it one more time for England' with a Bondmaiden in bed. Nor is there the forthright xenophobia of *Who Dares Wins*, in which Britain finds herself momentarily under threat from 'terrorists' (i.e. CND activists) whose leaders are triply alien: foreign, female and Red. In contrast to that film's circularity, epitomised by its opening and closing 'rhymes' (schematic images of the State: Big Ben, Churchill's statue, a London bobby), nationhood in *Chariots* is a dynamic thing, challenged by the interloper, yet remaining in essence unchanged. One recalls the conclusion to George Orwell's impassioned wartime essay, *England, Your England*:

> The Stock Exchange will be pulled down, the horse plough will give way to the tractor, the country houses will be turned into children's holiday camps, the Eton and Harrow match will be forgotten, but England will still be England, an everlasting animal stretching into the future and the past, and, like all living things, having the power to change out of recognition and yet remain the same.

Thus Janus-faced is *Chariots*. It looks both forward (Abrahams' prophetic announcement that 'the future lies with me') and back (the memory of the 'lost generation', the flower of British youth cut down in World War I, that haunts the film); and it can be both hailed as the vanguard of a 'new' British cinema and, in Puttnam's little trailer, quietly take its place in the 'Great Tradition' of that cinema's glorious past.

Abrahams with the Masters

*The Ploughman's Lunch* was, by contrast, intended from the start to be a portrait of Britain as she is now – a report on the 'temper of the times', in the manner of European art films like *The German Sisters* or *Man of Iron*, according to writer Ian McEwan and director Richard Eyre (*City Limits*, May 1983). Distinct from the timeless present of *Local Hero* or the costumed splendour of *Chariots of Fire*, *The Draughtsman's Contract* and *Gandhi*, Ian McEwan and Richard Eyre set out to delineate a more familiar, modern and metropolitan world, of Victoria-Line tube trains, squash courts, publishers' launches and smart wine bars (which cognoscenti could take additional pleasure in identifying by name). Concerned with the recent Falklands crisis, climaxing in the 1982 Conservative Party Conference (with Margaret Thatcher recruited as an unwitting extra and as the ultimate guarantor of a certain quasi-documentary realism) and released in London on the very eve of the 1983 General Election, *The Ploughman's Lunch* was perceived as unimpeachably up-to-the-minute. Small wonder that its proponents praised it as 'the most important film made in Britain and *about* Britain this last decade'.[5]

But, in spite of its state-of-the-nation status, *The Ploughman's Lunch* was placed by many critics just as firmly in a British *fictional* tradition – a sort of *Room at the Top* for the 1980s, with its main character, James Penfield (Jonathan Pryce), an opportunistic BBC news editor in quest of fortune through his courtship of rich bitch Susi Barrington (Charlie Dore) and fame through his planned book on the Suez crisis, appearing as a modern reincarnation of those kitchen-sink anti-heroes, and fascinated by the very same 'social and moral traumas which produced the Joe Lamptons and Jimmy Porters'.[6]

Thus, like *Chariots*, *Local Hero* and a host of others, *The Ploughman's Lunch* was endowed with an impeccably British cinematic heritage – a curious irony, perhaps, in the case of a film overtly and insistently out to expose the appropriation and manipulation of history. Early on, we hear that a forthcoming BBC radio programme will explore 'how the governments of Eastern Europe distort their past in history books to suit their present policies and allegiances', with obvious intimations that Penfield and his peers are busily engaged in very similar falsifications. This appears most crassly in his Suez book, which revises those events to chime with the Falklands factor: no longer a national humiliation, but the laudable defence of imperial honour. Penfield's method is to (re-)construct his story – history – from fragments of found experience: the knowledge of others, like Susi's mother (Rosemary Harris), or a university lecturer whose ideas are heard, now and again, in disembodied, dismantled snatches on Penfield's cassette recorder. It is history as *bricolage*. The same strategy is at work, more obliquely, in the scenes at the BBC, observing the production of the news – tomorrow's past: the film's first sequence, for instance, follows a telex of the 'South Georgia story', which is about to break, around the newsroom until it reaches Penfield, who is just then filing a report on some 'fifty or sixty scrap metal workers'.

Or again: a 'warm, loving, happy family' enjoying a bedtime drink in its snug 1930s home is unceremoniously invaded by a crew shooting a TV commercial, and Eyre's camera tracks around elaborately with James behind the set to discover two technicians spraying the windows with rain in the company of a black-and-white cut-out cow. It is the creation of instant, but ersatz history, just as, the ad director later (inaccurately) explains to Penfield, the 'ploughman's lunch' (bread, cheese and pickle), which lends the film its title, is not traditional olde English fare but an adman's invention of the 1960s to get people to eat pub grub. In short, yet another 'completely successful fabrication of the past'.

The effect is to show production 'frozen' into consumption, process into commodity, a fetishised past offered for sale in bookshops, over pub counters or on supermarket shelves. 'We might have led the world once into the Industrial Revolution', remarks the same director, 'but now we lead with television commercials.' Hence, no doubt, the immoderate emphasis in *The Ploughman's Lunch* on consumption, conspicuous to the point of gluttony, almost grotesquerie: expense-account eating at Langan's, absurd cocktails sipped through straws, champers to pass the time on the jaunt to Brighton, dyspeptic images of Britain's opinion formers, perpetually out to lunch.

They are themselves formed by their surroundings, though. 'I must say, they struck me as rather empty people,' observes Susi's mother, and they are indeed exactly that: mouthpieces – media, literally – for the messages their institutions purvey. Sometimes, it would seem, naively so, as when Susi reacts to archive newsreels of Suez, 'Why don't they make propaganda films like that any more?' More knowingly, one suspects, in the case of Tim Curry's knavish hack, spokesman for the journalism that gave us 'Gotcha!' the *Sun* headline when the Belgrano was sunk.

Strangest of all is Penfield, played by a theatrical actor of distinction, whom reviewers liked to describe as 'febrile' or 'intense' but who comes on here, in what must be a studiedly distanced performance, as a political chameleon with dead-eyed vacancy, soaking up and reproducing the colours around. He is a man without qualities, because without a past. The final scene, originally intended to be the toast with his publisher to History, pulls that theme instead, in the finished film, back to the private level: the funeral at which Penfield's personal origins (his mother), already symbolically negated by him, are actually buried while he, caught in a freeze frame, furtively consults his watch, anxious to move on again.

Disconcertingly, as McEwan himself bears out, *The Ploughman's Lunch* refuses the convention of rounded, complex characters:

> When I write fiction, I find myself more interested in psychological states, which I think is something that film doesn't do very well, or not with any great finesse, or with a great deal of pretension, and that when I undertake to write dialogue I seem instantly to be in another frame of mind... to want to take on themes that are more broadly political.[7]

Rather than being an offshoot of documentary or fictional realism,

107

the resulting film is in many ways – and in defiance of its down-stated, almost 'transparent' *mise en scène* – closer to a modernist, satiric tradition. Thus the broadly allegorical names of certain characters: Gold, the right-wing publisher; the wily adman, Fox; and, most markedly, Susi/Suez. Thus, too, the 'problem' of moral perspective, or rather the lack of it. There is no identifying with any of these figures, even the good brave ones like the poet and his followers, James's father or the peace-campers. Susi's mother (Rosemary Harris), a radical historian who has retired from the fray to cultivate her garden, is a very partial exception. They are all kept marginal to the institutional sources of power, and gently, but damningly mocked. 'I hoped,' avowed McEwan in that same inter-view, 'to make the audience laugh at the people at the poetry reading.' In so doing, he has maintained a massive, ironic distance from all concerned that has stuck in the throats of those who dislike *The Ploughman's Lunch*.

A moral position is to be sought, then, somewhere in the inter-stices between the characters, the silence between their voices, rather than in anything that is actually said. The film works on the principles, not of harmony, but of cacophony, not consensus but dissent. So Mrs Thatcher's 'spirit of the South Atlantic' speech, with its paean to national unity and resolve – 'the resolute approach' – is placed against the faintly echoing chant of demonstrators outside the hall and Penfield's confrontation with his perfidious friend inside.

Just as the film is concerned thematically with various versions, different fabrications on the past, so structurally its own history is consciously contrived. This is not a case, as one critic claimed, of being 'right in the midst of us, recording, witnessing, testifying to the truth of our times, as the artist sees it.'[8] Instead, snippets of 'contemporary reality' are taken and transformed into a different, more bitter pattern of meaning: the Greenham Common women, thanked in the closing credit yet treacherously held to ridicule by the film, or Thatcher's peroration, 'If this is tomorrow's generation, then Britain has little to fear in the years to come', heard over a big close-up of the petulant Penfield.

The images of Britain, and Britons, offered here are, then, quite alien to those in *Chariots of Fire*. National identity is not something organic, invested in exceptional individuals (nor, for that matter, is it innate to the 'folk', as it was in *Local Hero*). The 'British tradi-tion' is synthetic, just as the nation's subjects, in a vision that is anti-humanist almost to the point of misanthropy, are seen as empty vessels ready to be possessed of the discourses that surround them.

It is scarcely surprising that questions of 'Britishness' should have been so central to these two films made at an historical moment when notions of national unity were once again being dusted down and re-mobilised in the interests of political expediency. But their strategical role in the 'British film renaissance' is no less significant. 'It is not just as an industry but as a culturally defined entity that British cinema has steadily withered away over the past two decades,'[9] wrote one critic in 1980, voicing a widespread disenchantment. The early emergence of such self-consciously British films and the promise of more to come were key factors in inverting this popular perception of bankruptcy so rapidly and so radically and in re-establishing the British cinema as a 'culturally defined entity'. Welland's Oscar acceptance speech proclaiming the arrival of a veritable army and stating the existence of a 'movement' effectively *avant la lettre* paved the way for more regionally specific films such as Bill Forsyth's *Gregory's Girl*, which enjoyed substantial Stateside success later that same year.

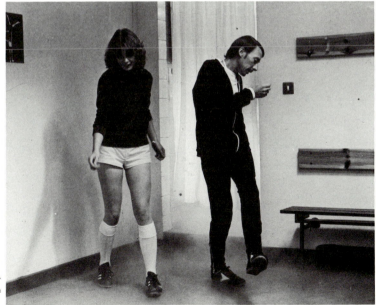

*Gregory's Girl*

However the British identity of both examples discussed here does not only reside at the level of their narrative concerns. They also draw, at the point either of production/marketing (the *Chariots* trailer) or of critical reception (the reviews of *The Ploughman's Lunch*) on powerful and long-established generic traditions within the national cinema, respectively historical costume fiction and the contemporary, socially aware 'kitchen-sink' drama. In each case, it has been argued, there are elements – of knowing self-parody or of modernist deconstruction – which lift the results slightly out of the rut of mainstream British realist cinema, lending them a complexity that perhaps helps to account for their interest and success. It is now to be hoped that subsequent films will continue to move away from hoary national mythologies and conventional narrative formats rather than safely choosing to reproduce the mixture as before.

# 9

# Reaching for the stars

An indigenous British cinema needs to have a distinctive
style of screen acting and a roster of bankable
box-office stars to attract audiences. With a few exceptions,
argues **Julian Petley**, British film acting has been
dominated by the theatrical tradition, yielding performances
that, by comparison with Hollywood, are wordy and
stagey, but there are signs of a new approach.

Throughout its history, the cinema has needed not just actors and
actresses but stars to sustain itself as a perennially captivating
mass entertainment. This was most spectacularly the case with
Hollywood in the great days of the studios, with their carefully
groomed contract artists, but it has also been true of other cinemas
– particularly if they were in competition with Hollywood for
national or international markets. There have been cinemas which
attempted to repudiate the notion of stars – Italian neo-realism for
example. But neo-realist films were rarely good box office, and it is
significant that the only neo-realist box-office success after 1948
was *Bitter Rice*, a star vehicle for Silvano Mangano and Raf
Vallone.

In the classic Hollywood system, the creation of a star was a
costly and elaborate process, which the studio attempted to control
in every minute detail. As David Kehr describes it:

It generally started with the selection of a 'type' – homespun or
sophisticated, glamorous or sincere – that would then be

elaborated through a steady accumulation of bit roles. At every step along the line, the screen image would be reinforced by a carefully controlled presentation of the star's 'private' life: features placed in the fan magazines, items inserted in the newspaper columns, the right gossip leaked at the right moment. By the time the performer was ready to graduate to leading roles, the distinction between on-screen and off-screen life no longer existed. Every new film was a chapter in an ongoing biography, a drama faithfully followed by millions of moviegoers. In one sense, the business of the studio publicist was the manufacturing of myths, the day-to-day, on-the-line job of creating epic figures, heroes and heroines that could operate across the field of an entire culture... These performers became, themselves, part of the culture, units of meaning that could be deployed in the complex system of signification that made up the art of Hollywood movies.[1]

This long slow build-up facilitated that dialectic of actor and role which is one of the chief defining characteristics of the fully-fledged star performance. To quote Edgar Morin in his pioneering study, *The Stars*: 'The star is the product of a dialectic of personality: an actor imposes his personality upon the heroes he plays, these heroes impose their personality upon the actor; from this super-impression is born a composite being: the star.' And again: 'A star appears when the interpreter takes precedence over the character he is playing... and when the character profits by the star's qualities on the mythic level.'[2]

Today the full panoply of the old star system has ceased to operate, along with the studio system with which it enjoyed a symbiotic relationship. But it does seem as if much of the aura, if not the structures, of the old 'system' of stardom still persists – and not just in the case of established figures such as Clint Eastwood, Burt Reynolds or Barbra Streisand but also in that of newer arrivals such as Richard Gere, Robert de Niro, Meryl Streep, Nastassia Kinski. And stars both old and new are still regarded as highly 'bankable' – properties who can and do command huge fees.

Even under the old star system, however, British actors always tended to remain in the shadow of their American counterparts and were frequently whisked off to Hollywood. Thus, even as far back as 1938 *Film Weekly* was complaining of 'British producers' lackadaisical neglect of the rudiments of a starring system'.[3] Things did not improve after the war either: until the end of the 1950s it seemed as if no British film was complete without at least one faded Hollywood star in a leading role. Then, at the very end of the decade, with the belated eruption of the 'Angry Young Man' syndrome into the cinema, actors such as Tom Courtenay, Rita Tushingham, Alan Bates and Albert Finney looked as if they might be going to provide the British cinema with its own gallery of genuinely indigenous contemporary stars. Today, in the light of the widespread national and international interest shown in the post-punk cultural watershed, one might reasonably expect the British cinema of the late 1970s and early 80s to have produced a suitably iconic gallery of new faces and presences expressive of the country's new-found image, particularly given the increasingly close links between the film industry and the music business – where, of course, today's *real* stars reside.

On the whole in the 1980s star figures emerge in areas of popular culture other than film – in television, in sport, in journalism and, most of all, in popular music – and film is just one place where their images are projected. Star-making, in the sense of the creation of an immanent, readable, meaningful image, still clearly persists in our culture, but the process is now carried out by carefully orchestrated *multi-media* campaigns. The music business, in particular, operates

Jordan in *Jubilee*

113

a star system every bit as well defined and tightly organised as that of the Hollywood studios in their heyday, manufacturing publicity and promotion which in turn services a whole secondary criticism/commentary/fan industry. Thus for *Picturegoer, Photoplay, Pictureshow*, substitute *Smash Hits, Chart Beat, No 1*; for *Sight and Sound, Stills, Monthly Film Bulletin*, substitute *The Face, New Musical Express*, and so on.

If one of the key defining characteristics of a star is the powerfully iconic connotations of his/her image – what one might call their charisma – then the only real stars which Britain has produced since the mid-1970s are Johnny Rotten/John Lydon, Sid Vicious, Siouxie Sioux, Sting, Boy George and Annie Lennox, none of whom (except John Lydon in *Order of Death*) have managed to

---

**A typical nineteenth-century Punch cartoon would show two people sitting at a table, with anything up to eight lines of dialogue under the drawing. Cartoons nowadays have quite a different emphasis and consequently more impact. Much of what is described as British cinema is still in the Victorian cartoon age.**

**Simon Perry, Producer**

---

transfer their images to the cinema screen with any degree ot success. Why should this be so, given that, for instance, American stars like Barbra Streisand, Liza Minnelli, Diana Ross and Debbie Harry of Blondie all arrived in the cinema direct from records and the concert stage? Perhaps one reason lies in the mushrooming video promo industry which finally satisfies record companies' craving for maximum visibility for their artists. However it should also be noted that video promos are themselves moving far beyond mere representation of performances into distinctly narrative territory, be it on the small scale – *Come Dancing* (the Kinks), *Under Cover* (the Rolling Stones) – or the large – *Mantrap* (ABC) – all of which were directed by Julien Temple. Increasingly, then, these too can be regarded as, indeed present themselves as 'films' in their own right. But, more specifically, the British cinema has always tended to turn towards the stage in search of new talent, and visitors from the world of rock music have not on the whole been well received. There is perhaps no better illustration of the stranglehold exerted over the British cinema by the indigenous literary/theatrical tradition, with its demands for conventionally 'well written' and 'well acted' films, than the failure of the critics to get to

grips with the truly mythic Presentations of Self by Bowie in *The Man Who Fell to Earth* and Jagger in *Performance*, neither of which were 'great performances' in the British theatrical tradition, but, rather, more 'Hollywoodian' explorations and invocations of star personae.

However, the new British cinema has not entirely bypassed the punk watershed and its aftermath: Julien Temple's Sex Pistols film *The Great Rock'n'Roll Swindle*, a wickedly ironic look at how modern stars (or rather 'anti-star' stars) are created, features not just the band itself but also arch punk-impresario Malcolm McLaren and eighties sub-culture heroes Mary Millington and Ronnie Biggs. Derek Jarman's *Jubilee*, too, featured a whole host of punk luminaries such as Toyah, Jordan, Wayne County, Gene October and The Slits. Jack Hazan and David Mingay's *Rude Boy*, an uncompromising drama-documentary set around The Clash, is the second part of a supposed diptych of contemporary British life (the first being the film on David Hockney, *A Bigger Splash*). This film and its 'stars' offer a more telling reflection of contemporary Britain than films from 'high-culture' sources like *The Ploughman's Lunch*. By contrast, *Breaking Glass*, with real-life 'punk' star Hazel O'Connor as an aspirant musician in contemporary London, seems tame indeed – all surface seediness, a carefully packaged, middle-aged ad man's view of the New Wave.

The new British cinema also includes various attempts to inject punk/New Wave stars into 'straight' non-musical roles: for example, Toyah in *The Tempest*, Sting in *Brimstone and Treacle* and *Radio On*, and Claire Grogan in *Gregory's Girl* and *Comfort and Joy*. 'Old Wave' stars Roger Daltrey and Adam Faith appeared in *McVicar* whilst *The Wall* represents a curious fusion of old and new waves with Bob Geldof, star of The Boomtown Rats, playing Pink in the film of Pink Floyd's mega-album. Stars of past and present also interweave curiously in another film of an album, *Quadrophenia*, Franc Roddam's fine visualisation of The Who's second and less famous 'concept album'. Set in the Mod era of 1964, its release coincided nicely with the Mod Revival, and offered a view of the sixties through an eighties prism. This feeling is much enhanced by a cast of unmistakably eighties faces including Toyah, Sting, Phil Daniels (*Breaking Glass, Scum*), Mark Wingett (*Music Machine, Breaking Glass, Fords on Water*) and Ray Winstone (*Scum, That Summer*).

Curiously, rather few television stars in Britain have transferred successfully to the cinema. This may be due to structural rather than specifically cultural factors, for although television tends to use the word 'star' to apply to chat-show hosts, newscasters, weather forecasters and actors alike, the medium actually fosters 'personalities' as opposed to stars proper. As John Ellis puts it in *Visible Fictions*: 'The personality is someone who is famous for being famous, and is famous only in so far as he or she makes frequent television appearances... In some ways, they are the opposite of stars, agreeable voids rather than sites of conflicting meanings.'[4]

The television experience is much less intense and more diffuse than the film experience: in television everything tends to be *smaller* than life. In particular television does not produce that play between the ordinariness and extra-ordinariness of its performers that characterises the Hollywood star system, both old and new. To quote Ellis again: 'The institution of television (at least in Britain) seems at pains to reduce the star phenomenon by reducing the extra-ordinariness of its performers, and their status as figures of an equivocal attraction and identification by viewers both male and female... Its stress is rather more on the ordinariness of its performers, using them with greater abandon than cinema could ever conceive, presenting them as much more of an immediate presence.' 'Likeability' appears to be the most important trait of the television actor – witness the success of Richard Briers, Michael Crawford, Felicity Kendall, Wendy Craig, Terry Scott, June Whitfield, etc. What seems to count above all with the television star is *human* quality, as Bruce Cook has noted: 'The personal style of the movie star becomes worth very little on television. What TV audiences (unconsciously) and producers (quite consciously) look for are personalities who fill the small screen comfortably... It is this human quality that makes an actor a star on television; he must be somebody with whom you can feel comfortable in your own home.'[6]

If television stars' main contributions to British cinema seem mainly to have taken the form of the dreaded TV spin-off movie, a select few have made considerably more impact. Foremost amongst these is Jeremy Irons, described in a recent issue of *Film Comment* as 'the first English actor to make an international breakthrough since the glory days of the sixties'. After a large amount of stage work Irons became more widely known through television in *Notorious Woman*, *The Pallisers*, *Love for Lydia*, *Langrishe Go Down*, *The Voysey Inheritance*, and, most memorably, *Brideshead Revisited*. The happy conjunction of *Brideshead* with his first major

Jeremy Irons and Stephane Audran in *Brideshead Revisited*

film role in *The French Lieutenant's Woman* has indeed led to Irons
receiving the full-blown star treatment right across the media both
in Britain and abroad (career profiles in heavyweight film magazines alongside gossip and scandal-mongering in the tabloid press).
To date his success as a star is principally founded on his
impersonation of a familiar English stereotype: a pre-World War
Two English gentleman, slightly decadent, preferably with an
ambiguous sexual identity. The fact that Rupert Everett has been so
sensationally successful in just such a role in *Another Country* (and
is quite clearly being groomed for star status on the strength of it)
suggests not so much the need for an English pin-up equivalent of
Richard Gere but rather the potent appeal of this particular
stereotype at the present moment, relating as it does to such
familiar English vices as nostalgia for the Imperial past, an obses-
sion with failure and humiliation, and a highly ambiguous fascination with the mores (especially sexual) of the upper classes. Apart
from the interesting image detour marked by *Moonlighting*, Irons
has continued his successful role as an upper class icon in *Betrayal*
and *Un Amour de Swann*, forging that consistent, slightly myste-
rious screen persona that is the mark of the star in the traditional
sense of the term. In particular the press's representation of Irons

Miranda Richardson and Rupert Everett in *Dance with a Stranger*

has generated that tension between the ordinary and extraordinary that separates the star from the mere actor.

In contrast, stars such as Julie Walters, Ben Kingsley and Bob Hoskins, whether they are appearing on television or in the cinema, are constantly represented, albeit in different ways, in terms of their *ordinariness*. Significant, in this respect, is Julie Walters' background in television prior to *Educating Rita*, where she is best known for her extremely fruitful partnership with Victoria Wood in *Talent, Nearly a Happy Ending* and the series *Wood and Walters*, although she also starred in the Alan Bennett plays *Me I'm Afraid of Virginia Woolf, Say Something Happened* and *Intensive Care*, and turned in her most striking television role as Angie (Chrissie's wife) in the 'Shop Thy Neighbour' episode of *Boys from the Blackstuff*. But if Walters' media persona is resolutely and consistently that of a scatty but down to earth Northerner, living in a two-room flat in Fulham and turning down lucrative offers of work in Hollywood, that of Ben Kingsley rests not simply on his ordinariness but, paradoxically, his unknownness: witness the headline of the *Womans Own* profile of 27 November 1982 'Ben Who?', or the subtitle of the *TV Times* feature on 26 February 1983 'Kingsley? Never 'eard of 'im!' Indeed, it is hard to resist the conclusion that

Kingsley's success in *Gandhi* lies not in the fascination of the star's persona but in his remarkable, self-effacing immersion – disappearance even – in his role (witness the relative *lack* of media flurry which greeted his performance in *Betrayal*).

Like Julie Walters, Bob Hoskins first attracted public attention for his television work – specifically in *Pennies from Heaven*. He then went on to repeat this success in the cinema with his role as

---

**British films today seem to me to fall into two categories. First there is the cinema of suffering. These films have a serious message, very few laughs, and are, quite often, less than fascinating to watch. Then there are films whose content may not be specifically British, but in terms of their attitudes and treatment would not have been made in the same way by anyone else.** *The Killing Fields* **is probably the best example in this category. This is a film that, had it been made by Americans, would have been treated in a very different way.**

**I believe that we should make some films dealing with parochial themes and which are very British in their attitudes. On the whole these will have to find their audience mainly in Britain and therefore by necessity should be low-budget pictures. It is sometimes possible for a film to be very British in its concern and still attract audiences abroad, but it has to have a very distinctive kind of appeal to a certain notion of Britishness.** *A Private Function* **is a good example of this category.**

**What is most important is the ability of the film really to involve the audience. It is vital, for without it we are lost.**

**Verity Lambert, Director of Production, Thorn-EMI Screen Entertainment**

---

the cockney gangster Harold Shand in *The Long Good Friday*. Again one finds that convergence between screen persona and off-screen media image ('The Bad Penny From Heaven', *Daily Mirror*, 7 April 1978), and a stress on ordinariness as a keynote of both ('Lovable Tough Guy', *Daily Mail*, 25 February 1981): like Harold Shand and Arthur Parker, Bob Hoskins constantly comes across as an ordinary bloke, a bit of a rough diamond, out for a lark, suddenly propelled into the limelight, an image perfectly summed up by the cover feature of *Time Out*, 5 March 1982: 'Bob Hoskins: Broke, Homeless, and the Hottest Property in Town'.

If there is no easily recognisable 'school' of new British film stars as there was in the sixties, there is an important connecting link between the various new names and faces of the British screen: their stage backgrounds. This joins not only the above but also Phyllis Logan (*Another Time, Another Place*), Stephen Rea (*Angel, Loose Connections*), Jonathan Pryce (*The Ploughman's Lunch*), Anthony Higgins (*The Draughtsman's Contract*) and Lindsay Duncan (*Loose Connections*). Significantly Ben Kingsley cut short the Oscar jollifications over *Gandhi* to return to London to perform *Kean* at the 500-seat Lyric Theatre, Hammersmith (a role he later recreated on Channel 4), whilst Bob Hoskins' next major success after *The Long Good Friday* was as Nathan Detroit in *Guys and Dolls* at the National Theatre (it being left to Hollywood to make the film version of *Pennies from Heaven*). What all this clearly reflects is not simply the paucity of British films but, more to the point, the enormous cultural sway still enjoyed by theatre in this country – an important aspect of the persistence of the primarily *literary* tradition of British culture, one which tends to result, in terms of cinema, in an excess of theatrical or literary adaptations or, in the case of original screenplays, scriptwriters' films.

The fact remains, of course, that the majority of British actors prefer or are obliged to return to theatre to stay in work. It is hardly

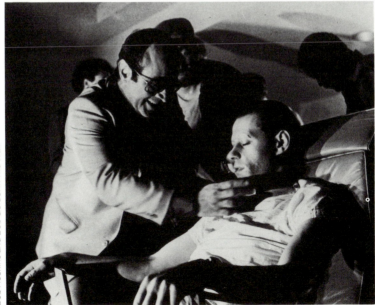

Bob Hoskins and Bob Geldof in *The Wall*

surprising, then, that film and television producers and casting directors continue to look to the theatre when casting films. Thus, compared with America, a greater range and number of actors in Britain are drawn from theatre backgrounds and bring with them a style of performance which is, in many cases, inimical to the demands of film representation.

Furthermore, because so much of the current British film industry is located in television, screen acting tends towards 'intimate' and 'low-key' styles which often seem at odds with the vestigial theatricality of the performers' backgrounds. Remarking on this problem recently, the British director Christopher Petit lamented the absence of actors who, in the Hollywood style, intuitively know how to *look* without appearing to *act*. If Britain is, at this late stage in the game, to boast a distinctive national cinema, and not just distinctive for its 'British' understatement, it needs to address the problem of performance. It is not so much the actors who have new things to learn. It is directors who, coming to feature film-making with either very little experience of directing actors or previous experience in the very different worlds of video promos, television and theatre, need to explore with their performers ways in which the *interacting* of camera and actor can generate more striking images.

# 10

# A critical impasse

Criticism plays a crucial role in the process of cinema, influencing audiences, making or unmaking the reputations of writers, directors and actors. **Steve Jenkins** castigates the British critical establishment for its failure to engage in serious debate about cinema and argues the case for seeing film criticism as an integral part of the context of British cinema.

In 1974, Barry Norman dismissed the Edinburgh Film Festival book on Raoul Walsh by hurling the publication across the *Film Night* studio floor. While this represents a novel approach to reviewing, it also points to a problem in any consideration of film criticism: that of defining the object in question. Is there any useful sense in which Arthur Thirkell's writings in the *Daily Mirror*, Stephen Heath's in *Screen*, and all points in between can be pulled together under some all-embracing heading? Or, as Norman's gesture suggests, are Thirkell and Heath involved in opposing practices, which need to be seen as such in order to make sense of either?

The alternative to such gestures is to construct an image of criticism in which a range of writings, of varying degrees of sophistication, 'quality' and interest, co-exist, interrelate, succeed and occasionally influence each other. Initially, therefore, I propose to consider a relatively recent and significant overview of the subject, which attempts precisely to circumscribe the spectrum, to pull disparate writings together in a manner which ensures that the resulting overall picture makes (common) sense. The article in question is 'The Critical Faculty' by Gilbert Adair, which appeared in the Autumn 1982 issue of *Sight and Sound*. It is a significant piece, partly because this was the 50th anniversary issue of what is generally considered one of the most important British film magazines, not simply in terms of longevity and 'quality', but because – as Adair puts it – '*Sight and Sound* has had to put up with a deal of adverse comment over the years, each new-minted magazine using it as the wall against which to play critical squash.' This actually suggests, it should be noted, that 'the road of British film critical writing', along which Adair, according to the magazine's contents page, is considering 'some markers', can, in part at least, be characterised by oppositions rather than simple flow and development.

In fact, Adair does take this into account. He deals with journals such as *Movie* and *Screen* in terms of the various forms of scorn and hostility they have provoked, citing the hysterical reaction on the part of the 'critical fraternity' to the interview with Minnelli which appeared in the first issue of *Movie*, and the more recent Kevin Brownlow/Lindsay Anderson affairs, in which *Screen* has served as a convenient punchbag. But what is interesting is the way Adair judges and places both the journals and the reactions to them within a scheme designed to resolve oppositions, to restore a sense of balance, presumably what the writer believes *Sight and Sound* readers require. Thus the Fleet Street critics are caricatured for their response to *Movie*, but the contributors to the latter magazine are similarly dealt with: 'Like most of the cinephile race, the *Movie* brats had a producer's cast of mind. Ideas were anathema to them'. In the same way, Brownlow and Anderson's anti-intellectual attacks on film theory and education are countered, but with a concomitant series of 'balancing' observations: 'In fact, *Screen*... has differed little in quality from other serious film magazines. It has published some interesting pieces... and a number of poor, even unreadable ones... Relatively few of the dissenters... had got close enough to structuralism... to judge it on a base other than that of prejudice. It was its bristly, cactussy surface which repelled them. And there, to be sure, they did have a point.' There is actually an important difference between these two examples. In the case of *Movie* and its detractors, both are considered negatively. With *Screen* and 'the dissenters', the two sides are merely counterposed, opposing positions with points for and against. It is as though historical distance allows a greater degree of dismissive cynicism, while events closer to the present require more delicate handling.

What is at stake in this distinction is that which is repressed from Adair's article: his own critical position and that of *Sight and Sound*. (Despite the usual 'signed articles represent the views of their author' disclaimer, it is impossible to read an article like this, in a 50th anniversary 'special', as anything other than a kind of disguised policy statement.) At one point, Adair states that 'it would be not quite plausible for me to discuss it [*Sight and Sound*] here.' But it seems not only plausible, but essential, particularly if the magazine is serving the 'squash wall' function which Adair claims for it. Certainly, other journals regularly acknowledge, state and define their positions with regard to various ideological options within film culture. And equally, it is impossibly misleading to discuss and dismiss *Movie*'s auteurist line without properly accounting for it historically as a polemic, which in turn requires an account of what the journal was reacting against, which would certainly involve consideration of *Sight and Sound*. Without this sense of oppositions and context, any critical position is only too easy to caricature and ridicule. This is especially true when your own attack comes from nowhere, from no identifiable position, from an ideal place somewhere outside every debate where both sides can always be grasped. Equally significant is the attempt to seal *Movie* off, paradoxically by talking about its influence ('negligible' on 'mainstream criticism', 'powerful' on *Time Out*). In fact, *Movie*'s importance lies not in its influence but in its place within the development in this country of film theory around authorship and the American cinema; as the starting point of a line taking in, for example, Peter Wollen's revisions in *Signs and Meaning in the Cinema*, the Edinburgh Film Festival's various director retrospectives, and, more recently, a debate around Joseph H. Lewis between Paul Willemen and Paul Kerr in the pages of *Screen*. Similarly, to talk about *Screen*'s 'quality' and the 'interesting pieces' it has published is to misrepresent the journal's significance. The latter *does* lie in its massive influence, particularly in the 70s, on the development and direction of film and television studies in Britain. In this sense, to claim that 'no one has as yet been bodily coerced into reading either Christian Metz or *Screen*' is misleading, since anyone entering the realms of film academia is more than likely to be subject to exactly such 'coercion'. But to broach the question of

125

influence in these terms would necessitate a proper account of the body of theory generated by the journal and its use within formal education (in order, presumably, to offer supportive or counter positions). But no, 'structuralism' is merely set up in vague and inadequately defined terms, in order to be pinned down, alongside C. A. Lejeune, Gordon Gow, *Movie, Time Out*, Alexander Walker, Barry Norman et al., as so many targets for the writer's wit, so many markers along the road.

It becomes clear from Adair's article that the 'critical road' option is actually unworkable; the disparate writings and discourses he describes are more usefully seen as a series of parallel but distinct routes within film culture, the natures of which are determined by specific factors. Because the article is predicated on a 'ship of fools' view of criticism, in which the whole enterprise is absurd, laughable and doomed (basically because of the fact of falling cinema attendances), then it is essential that differences be repressed, that the caricature should be all-embracing. The result is not only a misrepresentation and distortion of particular histories, but also a failure to deal with the increasing fragmentation of film culture as a whole, the way in which so much activity, in terms of production and consumption, cannot usefully be related to the decline of mass attendances at circuit cinemas. As Adair suggests at one point, 'every weekday... you will find more movie enthusiasts in the BFI library than in a West End cinema... Departments of Film Studies are booming everywhere, it almost seems as if more books about the cinema are being published annually than movies are being made.' It then becomes necessary to consider how this shift is reflected across and through different writings, whether it is the *Sun, Sight and Sound* or *Screen*. The exact role(s) and function(s) of the writings should become clearer as a result.

For the purposes of this piece, I will concentrate on the group of writers who are employed by major newspapers to cover new releases in a weekly column. Not only do they fit the bill as regards most people's idea of what a 'film critic' might be, but they also seem to occupy some neutral middle ground, placed somewhere between the trade press (being independent of the film industry) and the more specialised film magazines (which 'aren't for everyone', in the way that a newspaper column is supposed to be). Their role also seems relatively straightforward: with no particular axe to grind, but with taste and discernment, they bring an experienced eye to bear on whatever happens to be placed before them. They don't, ostensibly, write to champion causes (in the way that *Movie* writers championed authorship); they write because films are released and part of the release process is that the products are accounted for and assessed on behalf of their potential audience. Spectators are intended to find the columns useful as regards making choices about what they might wish to consume. They offer, as Derek Malcolm put it in his introduction to his 'Malcolm's Movies' season at the National Film Theatre, 'a consumer guide for the public'.

However, while Malcolm's definition is designed to be disarmingly commonsensical about how critics' work functions, it is quite possible to consider their role from a different perspective. One might, for example, look at the columnists in terms of the different political attitudes which inform their writings and how these affect their critical positions and methods: the liberal championing of Third World cinema by Malcolm in the *Guardian*; the increasingly right-wing stances adopted by Nigel Andrews in the *Financial Times* and Philip French in the *Observer*; the ironically personalised, apolitical nature of Virginia Dignam's reviews in the (Communist) *Morning Star*; etc. But this would tend to emphasise the gaps between the columns, to bolster – even if negatively – the individual personalities of the critics and their work. In order to gain some purchase on the institution of reviewing, it might be more profitable to quote Jean-Luc Godard, whose discussion with Pauline Kael on 'The Economics of Film Criticism' was published in *Camera Obscura* (No. 8/9/10). 'But don't you feel,' Godard asks, 'as a writer in a magazine, that you are part of the chain of the advertising business, and thus of the movie industry?... How can you write in a little column like that between two advertisements?... Even if you are not a *Time* critic (because *Time* is in the movie business too) you are still part of the industry. Making a newspaper is part of the industry, it's part of the culture.'

Godard's point is obviously a broad one, but it is also particularly relevant to the specifics of weekly film reviewing. There is a very real sense in which the reviewers do not work for their newspapers or for 'the public', but for the film industry. The content of their columns is dictated by the national press show list drawn up each week by the Society of Film Distributors (SFD), a trade organisation. This has various ramifications. The list itself incorporates an order of priorities which the columns tend to reflect. New releases from major companies (particularly those who are SFD members) tend to be allocated prime slots, i.e. early in the week, while more 'marginal' product (e.g. a BFI Production Board film, a revival, or a film trailing a season outside the first-run circuit) is shown at the tail end of the available time, and is probably granted a similar place in the columns (if mentioned at all). In addition, the film industry's publicity-generating machinery obviously works to guarantee certain films a 'newsworthy' profile before they are even offered to the press; the pre-existing status of these films is therefore merely perpetuated and extended by the press show/ review mechanism. Indeed, from the industry's point of view, the purpose of generating reviews is simply to produce more copy, whether favourable or not, around their product. The situation is reduced to its purest form, a kind of degree zero of criticism, when the reviews are quoted on posters, where the space separating obvious from disguised publicity is simply dissolved. It is entirely fitting that, at this point, the industry's publicists actually cut up the columnists' reviews to suit their needs. This makes nonsense, for example, of Pauline Kael's claim that 'I have *never*, ever, been asked to change an opinion, or to do anything to oblige advertisers'; of course not, the publicists will made any necessary changes. For example, a negative review of *One from the Heart* appeared in the *Monthly Film Bulletin* for June 1983, containing the following:

> One might uncharitably see *One from the Heart* as a promo film which all too clearly reveals the schizoid dream of Coppola's Zoetrope studios. Thematically (and choreographically), it is pure old-time romance... while visually it is a never-ending fizz of eye-blinding neon, surreal chromatic effects and infinitely extendable camera movement. *One from the Heart* is bursting with stylisation, but what it most sorely lacks is a style that could unite its human and technological elements.

The advertisement for the film which appeared in *Time Out* (8–14 July 1983) bore the legend: '"Never-ending fizz... bursting with style" MFB.'

All this might not be so significant if the columns did actually function as neutral consumer guides, albeit at the behest of the industry. But the fact is that the columns are also highly selective. Certain sections of the industry function quite happily without employing the services of the reviewers; their product is therefore not included in the columns. Sex, horror and other forms of exploitation cinema, for example, are regularly not previewed for reviewers and find their audiences while bypassing the critics. On the other hand, the newspapers themselves indulge in a concomitant practice whereby they choose to ignore, or else treat in a tokenist fashion, work and exhibition practices from outside the mainstream of the market/industry. (Until fairly recently, for example, the *Standard* had a *policy* of not covering openings at the ICA cinema.) What starts to emerge from this is therefore a kind of exclusive, demarcated middleground, somewhere between, say, the Moulin sex cinema and the London Film-Makers' Co-op, where reviewers are required to exercise their good taste.

This also implies, although it is never acknowledged, that the columnists are actually writing for a very specific sub-section of the public; the notion of 'the public' as an all-embracing, generalised body disappears, replaced by an imaginary being defined only by a lack of interest in soft-core and the avant-garde. Terms like middle-of-the-road, middlebrow, etc. might well come to mind. The proliferation of ways of viewing films, even merely of the kind the reviewers deal with, other than as isolated entities at first-run cinemas – on television, video, as part of seasons or film courses, etc. – also makes the specificity of the weekly reviewers' practice all the more apparent. In the case of television and video, the films themselves become to a degree subsumed into a wider flow of visual material which is regularly consumed. Similarly, with film seasons and courses, the films are contextualised in various ways so that their 'significance' or 'meaning' becomes subject to flux and shift. It is necessary to stress all these pressures, restrictions, omissions and specificities in order that the actual role of the columns should emerge, since it is exactly built into their practice that this should be disguised. The business of reviewing represents itself as a 'natural' process – an historical, seamless, regular encounter between reviewers and texts, which need never justify or explain itself, and which remains (somewhat like Adair/*Sight and Sound*) outside theory and debate.

Occasionally, films are presented to the reviewers which reveal, with particular clarity, the illusory, 'unnatural' nature of this position. The re-released 'missing' Hitchcocks are an especially good example. History intrudes here with a vengeance. The films in question are by a director who has been a constant focal point in the development of film theory, whether it be auteurist (Robin Wood), psychoanalytic (Raymond Bellour), structuralist (Peter Wollen) or feminist (Laura Mulvey). To pretend that the rediscovered films can be considered in isolation, separate from other Hitchcocks or the critical texts which have accrued to them, is clearly a nonsense, a misleading rewrite of a history. But from the start, the reviewers are compromised. In order to maximise profits from the re-releases, the films are offered to the public one at a time, and must be dealt with accordingly by the critics. In the case of *Vertigo*, the example to be dealt with here,[1] this meant that it was in most cases discussed alongside *Love Streams, Testament, Flight to Berlin* and *Risky Business*, the week's other new releases. This encouraged the reviewers to seal the film off, not to relate it to other Hitchcocks (apart from references to *Rear Window*, the only other title to have been re-released thus far, and mentions of *Marnie* and *Psycho*), but to use the small amount of space available to discuss the specific pleasures offered by this text. The film's history then becomes (re)written in a particular way. It becomes a question of then (when the film was not rated) and now, when it is (by some) and still isn't (by others). The latter viewpoint is timeless. Remarks such as 'Not the greatest Hitchcock, but you have to admire the craftsmanship', 'tantalising though slightly overwrought', 'the most preposterous of his psychological hokum', 'rather laboured and plodding' and 'had me dropping off from time to time', could have been written in 1958, despite occasional accompanying nods to the film's reputation. What separates then from now, and which should presumably inform and be acknowledged by current reviews, is not simply time, but the previously mentioned theoretical developments. But the reasons why reading a Hitchcock film is, or ought to be, of necessity a different matter in 1984 than it was in 1958 are glossed over, hinted at but not articulated. Thus, the film was 'no great success with the public in its day but since has been highly esteemed by connoisseurs, especially the French critics'. It 'returns in a blaze of glory, having been voted one of the 10 best movies of all time in *Sight and Sound*'s last international poll'. It 'is prized by film buffs'. These references refer, in effect, to the question actually posed by one of the reviewers: 'I am perhaps one of the few to be perplexed by the way these commercial entertainments, admittedly slick or sophisticated and certainly adroitly performed, that were not such sensations when originally released, should now be hailed to the skies as flawless.' This phenomenon can of course be explained, but the passing references to 'French critics' and 'film buffs' barely hint at the acute combination of auteurism and cinephilia which has given *Vertigo* its particular status. But instead of using the film to broach this issue, this history, the reviewers dodge the question, informing their readers merely that 'we're older, wiser... we can now see the skill'. In fact, readers are urged not to place any third terms (theory, history) between themselves and the screen. Instead, and crucially, 'you should clear your mind, fill it with intelligent suggestibility and *then* go out and see this gleaming masterpiece'. The important thing is exactly to reduce the experience of seeing the film to basics, the encounter between a 'clear mind' filled with 'intelligent suggestibility' and a 'master-piece', with no Wood, Bellour, Wollen, etc. to get in the way. In other words, this is a more understated version of the Barry Norman/Raoul Walsh syndrome. This attitude is a means of pulling into place a film which doesn't fit too easily within the province of the column, because its critical significance spills over. But this significance is repressed as the gap between then and now is closed; the film is nostalgically juxtaposed with present-day product in terms of 'quality'. Though 'never the best of Hitchcock... It is still a good deal better than anything else that may currently be seen around'; 'they don't make films like that any more, and the more they try the more they fail'; we are 'poorer by far in the kind of entertainment *Vertigo* represents'. The fact that the film was the first to be presented at the Electric Screen, after the demise of the Electric Cinema Club, enabled the reviewers to close the circle even more tightly, locking the film into a nexus of nostalgia, pleasure and individual taste which the screening venue itself confirmed: it is cited as 'just the right setting for this nostalgic reissue'; '*Vertigo* will doubtless prove a dizzy delight for buffs and nostalgics and it is certainly an inspired choice to launch a new art house catering to London's discriminating cinemagoers.'

Because *Vertigo* has a pre-existent critical history and context before it reaches the reviwers, their reaction – repress all this in favour of the individual, untainted response – is all the more clearly a reflection of the industry's model for film consumption (single works sold on the basis of specific pleasures, with no contextualisa-tion other than what is productive in marketing terms). The reviewers' position emerges by default. With most releases, which lack a similar history, what's being repressed from reviews is not always so apparent. The commonsensical mode of address, from one person of taste, discrimination and discernment to another, is intended to aid the wrapping-up of the product within the limited space of the column. This requires the film to be placed (so that the reader knows what kind of object it is) and then evaluated (whether it succeeds on the terms preordained by its status). This marketing function, of describing and rating possible pleasures on offer, can again be related to the middle ground with which the columns deal. With sex films, for example, the product is usually 'placed' precisely by its exhibition outlet, in a 'sex cinema', where customers are fully aware of the pleasures being purchased with the admission ticket (much like an art house in fact). The services of reviewers simply aren't required for this kind of product, since the notion of evaluation is clearly problematic. Or rather, it is all too simple: one sex magazine brilliantly encapsulated the reviewing process described above when it rated films according to the number of erections they inspired. Similarly, works which make demands on their audience different from those made by mainstream narrative cinema are likely to be excluded from the kind of distribution/exhibition sector within which the reviewers work.

What is so frustrating about their handling of films inside this area, however, is that everything is made to seem so transparently clear, so unproblematic; the wrapping-up process allows for no doubt, contradiction or leakage. But the terms by which the films are being packaged and judged for readers are concealed, implicit; they may well be inappropriate for a particular film, but since they are not being articulated anyway, the whole process retains its seamless air. Take, for example, Christopher Petit's *Flight to Berlin*, which was press-shown in the same week as *Vertigo*. The film is chiefly interesting because it invokes a whole series of pairings and oppositions. It was made by a director who started as a critic. The funding was mainly German, but with some British (BFI Production Board) money involved. Petit seems to be a British director with a particularly European 'sensibility'. The film is essentially an art movie (it opened at the Camden Plaza, an art house), but is also, almost, a thriller. *Flight to Berlin* could therefore be used to raise questions about cine-literate/philiac film directors, about what constitutes our sense of a British film or film-maker, about the relationship between 'art' and 'genre', etc. And these issues are occasionally mentioned across a series of largely unfavourable reviews.[2] But they are not raised in order to render the film, or the reviewers' positions, problematic. On the contrary, they are used to pin both film and director down, stirred in with a selection of arbitrary value judgments intended to suggest a common ground occupied by critic and reader. Thus, the film lacks the following:

rounded, flesh and blood characters (they are 'un-persons', they have no 'passion or intensity' or 'adequate human interest'), originality ('it is all déjà vu', 'its style and content are passé') and naturalistic dialogue (it is 'clotted with unspeakable lines' and 'portentous dialogue' with 'little wit'). There is a 'failure to evoke any emotion at all, at least in me'; 'there is no tension in the action'; 'the film is guilty of symbol quilting without adequate human interest'; the audience is limited to those 'who share his [Petit's] preoccupations', etc. The reviews can be reduced to a string of such judgments, which invite only their reverse: opposite values desired by a spectator who is the reversed mirror image of the composite reviewer. This spectator would not require 'convincing', 'passionate' characters, naturalistic dialogue, originality(?!), the invocation of emotion, tension or human interest. And s/he might well share Petit's preoccupations. And, according to the closed system of the reviews, such a spectator would not be addressed by the reviewers. It is exactly because Petit's film seems to fall between several stools, and because it is and is not a 'narrative' about 'characters', that is seems to elude the critics' grasp. Because it cannot be easily pigeonholed/packaged – like, for example, *Swann in Love* or *Sudden Impact* – its interest as the site of several disjunctures (and therefore the question it poses for *cinema*) goes unremarked.

Petit's film also raises, by default, the question of how these

Eddie Constantine and J.F. Stevenin in *Flight to Berlin*

critics relate to the supposed British Renaissance or Revival. The gulf between the way *Flight to Berlin* works and the demands made on it by the critics suggests how firmly placed they are within a liberal cultural mainstream (by which I mean one where 'human interest' is still of crucial importance). This is clearly helpful to the kind of renaissance being touted by such public figures as David Puttnam or Richard Attenborough. This is always seen either in terms of selling the audiences British rather than Hollywood product or of halting the decline in cinema attendances. Both these options involve an almost total emphasis on the territory marked out by the SFD press show list and the critics. Flags are waved around *Chariots of Fire* or *Gandhi* but the relationship between this flag-waving and the activities of film-makers such as Petit, Derek Jarman or Ken Loach is never explored. The fragmentation of British film culture is not a guarantor of column-inches, whereas a renaissance... The result is often fairly equivocal – support tempered with a degree of cynicism – but there is never any real questioning of exactly which cinema is being revived, or how a mythical national cinema might relate to an increasingly nebulous national identity.

If one wishes to examine the positions underpinning the reviewers' work, it is necessary, in order to find them expressed explicitly, to look outside the weekly columns. The *Critics' Choice* seasons[3] at the National Film Theatre are revealing in this respect. It is hardly surprising, given that the reviewers generally serve as functionaries of a marketing sytstem, that the seasons should be characterised by an extraordinarily dominant sense of self-assertion (starting with the portrait stills of the critics, as though they were stars in themselves). However, this actually reflects back on, and illustrates, their strategies within the columns: the notion of the ideal encounter between the clear mind and whatever is on screen; the absolute rejection of film theory (not one reviewer raises a single theoretical issue as such); the assertion of taste; the idea that films are judged according to their intrinsic 'quality' rather than as to how they might be used in understanding the institution of cinema. The key term is 'private pleasure' or 'private enjoyment', evoked when one decides that it is 'fatal to reflect. Better to let memory drift'. The films selected are 'simply some of my favourites... films of which the memory grows fonder'. Because 'critics are subjective creatures... the list says as much about me as about the cinema'. It refers to my 'Henry Fonda Syndrome: an abiding compulsion to

find myself in a minority of one'. The films can only be recommended to 'the "odd" people... who share my view of things'. Because of the lack of any perspective outside the sense of self, 'the choice becomes irrational' with no 'cohesive logic, except in the most general terms'. Film history becomes chaos as 'the titles knock at memory not by the dozen but by the hundred'. Understanding this history is a matter of knowing the 'great historical classics' and 'the masterpieces of the period'. These, however, do not always coincide with the demands of 'indulgence in revived pleasure' and it is important 'not to do the absolutely obvious. Masterpieces are there, but it's not the name of this particular game'. This is 'an aristocratic pleasure', where it is better in your monomania to 'choose heresy as a preference', while asserting your willingness 'to be judged by your choices'. The latter idea encapsulates the whole process perfectly. The films are selected in order to illuminate the figure of the critic, who can then be judged according to how well his or her taste matches that of the imaginary spectator. But what actually happens is that the selections come adrift from the introductions, the possible choices of any of the critics. The notes are sometimes distinguished by an acute sense of nostalgia, or a kind of right-wing, naughty-boy playfulness, which would enable one to identify the reviewer in question, but much more striking, in terms of what the films signify for their champions, are the similarities across the seasons. Films are, for example, 'vibrantly and unforgettably human', 'a paean to human dignity', 'illuminate the schematic with humanist concern'. They are 'mesmerising', 'dazzling', 'haunting', 'stunning', 'magical', 'intoxicating'. This plethora of mystificatory terms suggests that the ideal critical state is one where analysis is suspended in the face of a surfeit of private pleasure; the sexual analogy is evoked by the use of 'breathtaking' and 'you catch your breath'. It is no accident that these terms are exactly those which are plucked from reviews to provide advertising copy, confirming the reviewers' firmly fixed place within the institution they purportedly stand outside.

An alternative to all this is suggested by another season in the same series: a group of films chosen by Colin McArthur, one-time film critic for *Tribune*, a socialist weekly newspaper. The season is overtly distinguished from its predecessors by McArthur, who sees 'film reviewing (and the equally important job of discussing books, journals, and TV programmes about the cinema, as well as the workings of bodies like the BFI and the NFFC) as part of a *political* process – the interrogation of the institution cinema from a left perspective'. This declaration of an explicit position on the part of the critic is matched by an idea of a specific kind of spectator: 'film workers and audiences on the left' (as opposed to 'the public'). And the films are shown in order to pose the question: 'What can we learn from them?' This is the very basic but crucial difference between McArthur's and the other seasons. Alexander Walker, for example, offers an explicit (right-wing) political position, but the films are then merely read as expressions/embodiments of values/ positions with which Walker is in sympathy. It is the closed circuit again: the critic and what is on the screen reflecting and confirming each other with no space in between for any third term. McArthur, on the other hand, uses the films to suggest alternatives to the realist forms which he sees as dominating British film production, thereby offering an opportunity to consider issues of theory and practice as they relate to 'the "dream ticket" – left political analysis and optimum cinematic pleasure'. In effect, the point of his season is to cause himself to disappear in favour of this issue; the other seasons exist merely to provide captions for the photographs of their presenters.

Nevertheless, support for McArthur's critical position in this NFT context has to be qualified when considering a possible 'dream ticket' for film reviewing. McArthur's writings for *Tribune* have been collected in the book *Dialectic!*, and it is very noticeable that somewhere between the cover and the title page, the volume's sub-title mysteriously changes from 'Left Film Criticism' to 'Left Film Journalism – A Selection of Articles'. 'Criticism' suggests writings on individual film texts, while 'journalism' evokes coverage of the 'institution cinema', or film culture, in a much wider sense. The uniqueness of McArthur's column lay in its attention to the latter function (writings on *Film Night*, film board games, a *Framework* magazine conference, etc.), but the book is divided exactly between those pieces and the reviews of single films. The significance of film reviewing as practised by other columnists lies in the perpetuation of this distinction. The idea is maintained that what counts is the endlessly repeatable encounter between the spectator and the single text. McArthur was presumably able to displace this function because of the nature of the journal for which he was writing. But that any mainstream British newspaper should threaten its own, perfectly functioning place within the system outlined by Godard is unthinkable. In addition, McArthur's column frequently had the air of a left-wing head beating itself against a reactionary wall, with no hope of ever making any impression. The interface between much film theory, particularly of the 70s *Screen* variety, and notions of pleasure, in which mainstream reviewing clearly places a huge investment, is a difficult one, and McArthur's somewhat blunt, humourless and often hectoring approach never solved this problem. The real 'dream ticket' must lie elsewhere, ideally in some film equivalent of what happened to popular music in 1976 – a seismic shake-up at the level of 'production values' which forced a complete exposure and reappraisal of stale critical values. Except, of course, that the cinema's modes of production, distribution and exhibition will never be susceptible to such an attack...

Meanwhile, the very concept of a film culture, fragmented in itself and in terms of audience(s), will continue to be excluded from the review columns, both by the regular flow of product to be dealt with (which dictates the role of the columns) and by the monolithic resistance of the reviewers to any critical approach other than the narcissistic application of personal taste and sensibility. Which is not simply to endorse Gilbert Adair's view, obviously correct, that 'film reviewing in Britain has hardly budged in over three decades', but rather to insist that a lack of change is built into the prescribed role and function of film reviewing. Film culture shifts; the middle ground holds.

# 11

# Strengths
# and signposts

American investment is crucial to British film-making,
but the myth of the 'dominant dollar' is often a smokescreen
for a poverty of imagination on the part of the British
industry. 'Revivals' come and go, but when the enthusiasm
of creators coincides with good prospects
for investment a renaissance can perhaps be said to
be on the cards. **Quentin Falk** examines the state of play
in the pound vs. dollar stakes.

The British Cinema has known years of greed, restrictive practice, self-interest and sheer complacency. It has invariably been
disregarded and written off by successive governments despite its
enormous potential to be a vibrant industry. And yet this same
industry simply refuses to be consigned to a premature burial. In
fact the industry has 'died' so often over the past 50-odd years, that
it may be deemed, to borrow a vampiric analogy, to be a rather
lively zombie.

That the grave-diggers and the stake-wielders tend to come from
within the ranks is, I suppose, ironic but, in fact, historically
unsurprising. The very fragmentation of the UK industry has, over
the years, presented such a disunited front that it must have been
difficult for any government, let alone a fairly apathetic public, to
give any credence to a 'British film industry' with the unity implicit
in that phrase. Add to this a self-flagellatory attitude from critics
and film-illiterate media, and no one – from producers to cinema
managers, via the unions – can be immune from criticism.

So what is British cinema good at? Not self-advertisement, that's for sure. It is necessary, first, to counter the line of pure cynicism: 'Whenever the word "renaissance" crops up in the context of British Cinema, the chances are that the film industry is in deep trouble' (Thomas Elsaesser, *Sight and Sound*, Autumn 1984) and second, to challenge illogical, not to say reckless, generalisations: 'Every couple of decades, a revival is loudly proclaimed by those who work in the British film industry; and for a time, it seems as if the impoverished medium is finally about to become a creative, stimulating, and – above all – self-supporting industry. But in the past, each glimmer of hope has died in the suffocating clinch of tempting American finance and a severe lack of available home support' (Sally Hibbin, *Stills*, February–March 1984). This enervating mixture of the cynical and the syllogistic is hardly conducive to a climate of confidence.

The American influence is nothing new and in fact its perennial introduction into the debate as some kind of hobgoblin is frankly prosaic. By 1909, American films were dominating British screens and not long after, American-originated finance was beginning healthily to underscore British-based film production. Those who complain that American distributors have an excessive stake in British film production, or that Britain places undue reliance on American money, argue that if the Americans for some reason decided to withdraw from financing films in this country, this might seriously upset the British film production industry and perhaps cause it to collapse altogether. The argument goes on: if production finance were found to replace the (departed) American funding, there would then be a serious loss of talent, since actors, producers, directors and technicians would have followed the American distributors to America or to some other country.

The truth is, the Americans have regularly 'pulled out' – notably at the end of the 1960s when the vein of Swinging London had been successfully, and rather less successfully, mined – without complete collapse following in the wake. In an internationally based industry, in which America remains the single most potent force, there is surely nothing sinister about creative talent being drawn from all corners. The fact that British directors, from Tony Richardson to Alan Parker via a whole clutch of television journeymen are tempted periodically to ply their craft away from these shores ought to be preceived as a strength rather than as some kind of catastrophic irreversible 'exodus'.

The key phrase in the preceding argument is, of course, 'undue reliance' and it would be naive not to concede that the 'American influence' has not been without its considerable disadvantages. As the most prolific English-speaking production industry, with the matchless ability to 'travel well', its product serviced at times indiscriminately by distributors and exhibitors, Hollywood has swamped the market-place. American financing of British-based film-making has regularly resulted in compromise, loss of independence and the creation of the ugly, unwieldly, mid-Atlantic hybrid.

But while America may point to the vibrancy of its market – box office gross increased 46.6% between 1980 and 1984, to $4.03 billion, while ticket sales leaped 17.4% in the same period, to $1.19 billion last year – it is worth noting rather less encouraging statistics such as the negative cost of a feature film which rose from an average $11.9 million in 1983 to $14.4 million in 1984 – a quantum leap compared with the small rises in the preceding years. Also, the Motion Picture Association of America now reports, eight out of ten movies produced do not recoup their cost from domestic theatrical release and six out of ten do not make it into profit even with foreign and ancillary sales. But such an unpromising balance sheet does not faze the Americans because the cinemagoing habit is retained and even the number of screens is on the increase – up 6.9% in 1984 to 20,200.

The American majors spread the risk by producing large programmes of films and, at the same time, remain hand-in-glove with the ancillary media because the relationship, from production to distribution, can be absolutely complementary. Deregulation has become a strength in America and given that a similar climate is becoming apparent in Britain, the current weakness whereby the various media seem at odds with one another must be reversed if a film industry, in its widest context, is to forge ahead here.

It is generally believed that Britain is a very slow maturing market but as it matures, it will find growing opportunities for investment linked to deregulation. A three-fold technological deregulation, through video (levelling out after a phenomenally swift implementation), satellite (in its infancy) and cable (currently stuttering but expected to come again) has to be viewed in context with economic policy and Government impetus to move further to deregulate state monopolies.

With these cornerstones, and given an atmosphere of mutual

understanding, there should be no reason, many people argue, why Britain cannot look to the 1990s as the leader of Europe in the production area. Addressing itself to 700 million English-speakers around the world, Britain *can* provide the complementary alternative to America. Inevitably this rather glib scenario is studded with 'ifs' particularly when one considers how long it took to break down even something as fundamental to film-TV interrelationships as the five-year bar. The Americans very swiftly discovered that the very best way of promoting film was breaking down the barriers

---

**Having just returned from Los Angeles and the experience of sitting through innumerable repetitions of the same American teen movie, I am once again struck by the comparison with the tremendous amount of talent and innovative ideas that the British cinema has to offer. The confines of the American studio system and the problems of raising finance mean that no risks are taken and formula movies prevail. By contrast, the originality and the scope of the subjects now being tackled by the best of British cinema have no equal anywhere in the world, and Britain has every reason to be extremely confident about its place in world cinema.**

**A new breeze will be blowing through the British exhibition scene when American Multi Cinemas open the first of their ten-screen complexes in Milton Keynes at the end of 1985. No doubt the British circuits will be looking to their laurels.**

**Romaine Hart, Distributor**

---

between the media which also helped to increase film awareness. When Lord Grade unilaterally smashed the five-year 'rule' in Britain, he was decried as some sort of self-destructive force aiming to undermine the industry. Now happily there seems to be an altogether more flexible arrangement which, given broader application, can be moulded into a strength for the future.

When Gary Dartnall, head of the Thorn-EMI film operation and chairman of that well-meaning promotional binge British Film Year, purrs: 'British film production is booming. All of our studios are full and have bookings many months ahead. Our technicians are rightly regarded as the best anywhere and our facilities are permanently in demand', it should not be dismissed as meaningless public relations hype.

It is now a matter of record that the combination of indigenous theatrical and television production and American production based here has seen dubbing theatres, laboratories and studios working at capacity. A glance across the studio spectrum for 1984 and the early part of 1985 yields more than forty titles. In particular, at Pinewood: *Legend, King David, Steaming, Morons from Outer Space, Dream Lover, A View to a Kill, Santa Claus, Deceptions, D.A.R.Y.L., Spies Like Us, Horror Movie*; and at Shepperton: *The Company of Wolves, Ellis Island, Passage to India, Water, The Bride, Reunion at Fairborough, 2084, The Doctor and the Devils, Absolute Beginners.*

So the evidence of a boom and investment in indigenous creative and technical talent is clearly there. But is it merely self-deluding?

It is not just altruism that keeps production dollars flooding in; an advantageous exchange rate whereby the pound has plummeted well over fifty per cent against the dollar in the past four years helps and is likely to keep on doing so; lower labour costs, too, are often cited as an integral part of this transatlantic love affair. The issue of lower wages is, however, disputed by the British Film and Television Producers Association. At the top level, British technicians get the same as their American counterparts; at the average level, the difference is no more than fifteen per cent, says the BFTPA. The real savings, it adds, come from a 'realistic' attitude on the part of the unions compared with the wildly inflexible approach from, say, the Teamsters in the United States.

The American influence may have brought about occasional compromise, loss of independence and an inability, or unwillingness, by British producers to match 'top dollar' paid out by US employers but what has resulted is a broad and deep pool of resources, both human and technical. It is worth noting that when the case for an explosion of indigenous production is mooted, the much-vaunted Australian experience is carefully examined. The most recent film-making boom Down Under exposed a dangerously shallow pool of talent which, combined with a public apathy for Australian-made movies save the odd *Man from Snowy River*, curtailed activity. Britain at least has it half right.

These are merely the elements that underline a fundamental problem for British cinema, as opposed to British production in its broader-based service industry guise: lack of continuous investment, talent working in isolation with only sporadic and generally unimaginative corporate input. It is curious too that a Government which seems to claim some credit for 'freeing' the industry from bureaucratic entanglements withdrew the very encouragement that seemed to signal the possibility of self-support. The changes in the capital allowances will, it is predicted, reduce production by a third and, considering that around £210 million was invested in film-making here last year, that is a very substantial dent indeed. It also undermines, as if critical and media self-flagellation were not enough, the confidence shown towards film by the business community which has numbered such disparate film investors as Marks and Spencer, the Heron Group, C. E. Heath (insurance brokers), Ladbroke's, Bernard Sunley (building) as well as more conventional outfits like Barclays and Lloyds.

And yet a degree of continuity persists, against all the odds, from production houses such as Goldcrest, Virgin, Palace and Hand-Made while 'umbrellas' like Greenpoint, Quintet and United British Artists go on fostering talent. Can it still be for the chance of following in the footsteps of a *Chariots of Fire* or *Gandhi*, despite the fact that both these films have been re-evaluated in the wake of Oscar awards and international success, as 'mid Atlantic' and 'valueless'?

Thomas Elsaesser notes: 'Stylistically, the weaknesses of British cinema are intimately connected with its strengths: the close alliance with the theatre – whether one thinks of acting, writing or directing – and now the quite inextricable dependence of both theatre and the cinema on television, which of course is a mutual and a three-way relationship. What perhaps is missing in Britain is a film culture from the grass roots up or, equally important, a generation of not only cineliterate but genuinely cinephile writers and directors.' Historically, Elsaesser is correct but with the emergence of new, instant arts like commercials and video-promos, there has proved to be a crossover of talent with some genuine cinematic flair emerging. Lack of passion in scriptwriting, a vague embarrassment in trying to relate to real cinema, and limited ambition in the scale of production will always dog the British *modus*, but while there are producers like David Puttnam, Jeremy Thomas, Simon Perry, Alan Marshall, Mark Shivas, Simon Relph and John Goldstone, the job of nurturing a new generation of film talent is in imaginative, and thick-skinned, hands.

And yet the question must still be asked: what is the point of British Cinema if there is not a British cinemagoing audience to support it and, in any case, should a national audience necessarily be regarded as the 'bread and butter' for national product? The debate seems barely worth pursuing given the putrid state of distribution and exhibition in Britain today.

Just 1300 screens (ABC with 296, Odeon with 198, Classic with 132 and Star with 106 comprise the four largest units) in 700 sites, less than half the number in any other major European market; indifference to the customer and reluctance to spend money; conversions done on the cheap; failure to get out new pictures fast and wide thanks to the monopolistic practice of 'barring'; forced queues; the appalling physical state of cinemas plus lowgrade manpower; inaccessibility. A bizarre catalogue of complaints, particularly if one accepts the theory that film production can only realise its full potential if there is a healthy exhibition base in the home market.

After years of colluding in this folly, the industry finally, maybe miraculously, has conceded that it actually has a responsibility beyond merely pushing out marketable products on an indiscriminate basis. That dreadful film industry cliché about 'they'll come out for the right picture' has a hollow ring looked at in the context of the lowest ever cinema admissions. Films are no less 'right' than they have ever been in the past, and yet it is just past the eleventh hour for film exhibition in Britain.

This awareness, belated though it is, may become a real strength, indeed a signpost, for the future. Not only are the three main

Brazil

145

cinema chains spending more than £12 million on refurbishment and modernisation but plans are well ahead for multiplex leisure centres sponsored by new names in the British market like American Multi Cinema.

There is then, a climate of realism. Talent is abundant. Economic and common sense dictate that the current conflict and competition between the media must and will give way to financial and creative symbiosis. Under the circumstances, the future may not be as bleak as so many have painted it.

The *Kinematograph Weekly* editorial of 9 September 1941 might have been writing about 1985 when it asked:

> What is the real desire of the kinema patron? If anybody takes the trouble to inquire he will find it is to get away from the whole nasty business for a couple of hours – to live in another world and build up resistance to the wearying anxieties of the day by enjoying a spell of make-believe.
>
> Call it 'escapism' – why not? What else is there in any form of mental relief from hard conditions outside? And so long as the world can get this relief, however, temporary, so long is the kinema doing a good service.

For British 'kinema', that could be regarded as the bottom line.

# 12

# But do we need it?

In this final chapter, **Geoffrey Nowell-Smith** raises
some searching questions about the future of 'British cinema'
in a world where film production is increasingly
international and where film viewing takes place mostly
in front of the TV screen. The crucial issue,
he contends, is not whether British films will continue
to be profitable but what the future place of cinema will be
in popular cultural life.

Do we really need a British cinema? There is nothing rhetorical
about this question. It is perfectly serious. Up until a few years
ago such a question would not have had to be asked. There was a
British cinema. It may have been economically precarious and
culturally undistinguished. But it existed. It existed in the form of a
film-making infrastructure, a certain level of 'indigenous' production, a business (dominated by the Rank/EMI duopoly and the
American majors), a box office in excess of 100 million cinema
admissions a year, and a fairly thriving film culture. There was a
status quo which nobody was terribly happy with, but most people
accepted; and successive governments were committed to maintaining and perhaps improving it.

Since 1980 all this has changed. There is now an imminent
danger that British cinema, as we know it, will have effectively
ceased to exist within the decade. Ironically, there are probably
now more film-makers producing interesting commercial films than
at any time for the past thirty years. But the structures into which

these films can be inserted are fast falling apart. Cinemas are closing. Admissions look like dropping below 50 million (that is to say, less than one visit to the cinema per person per year). Britain is increasingly uninteresting as a market, and production is kept going because of the low level of the pound sterling, which makes the country useful as an off-shore base for the 'multi-nationals' (alias Americans). Video, broadcast TV and (in the offing) cable are becoming the preferred mode of diffusion of films: preferred by a stay-at-home public and a business eager to supply it. To today's children, 'film' is something on TV slightly different from the rest of TV. The death of traditional cinema (highly likely) and its trans-

---

**I see the British Film Institute as playing a vital part in encouraging film. Both through the National Film Theatre in London and throughout the country, the Institute ensures that as many people as possible have access to a wide range of films, both old and new.**

**Through the National Film Archive, the British Film Institute is also the protector of our film heritage. But the Institute looks to the future as well as the past. It produces valuable films, containing new ideas and approaches. Such original thought is very important, if the cinema in Britain is to survive as an industry and as an art form.**

**Lord Gowrie, Minister for the Arts**

---

formation into a new techni-culture (speculative) is seen by the Government as a natural development which should not be hindered by state interference.

Under the circumstances it becomes extremely pertinent to ask the embarrassing and hitherto rarely asked questions: What is British cinema, and who needs it? If British cinema is falling apart, it is important to establish whether it's worth trying to put it together again, and in what form?

What 'British cinema' is – its components and how they relate – has been fairly comprehensively dealt with in the foregoing essays in this book. The confines of British cinema traced in this book stretch from Wardour Street to the Regional Film Workshops; they take in television both as producer and diffuser of films; they include exhibition to British audiences of films of different national origins; and they allow for that essential difference between the cinema industry and most other industries, which is that its

148

products exist to be part of culture. Within these broad and shifting confines, however, certain internal boundaries need to be drawn and distinctions made. In particular it is important to distinguish very sharply, within the totalising and often misleading concept of British cinema, between 'British films' (however and wherever shown) on the one hand and 'cinema in Britain' (whatever the origins of the films shown) on the other. It is also important to distinguish – and this would apply to cinema anywhere – between the economic and cultural aspects of both film-making and cinema-going. Although every film is a cultural product (and even the decision to invest in a film is a cultural decision, an assessment of the state of cultural values as mediated through the marketplace), it is – to be quite blunt – only with certain films and a certain type of cinema that 'culture' becomes a plea of mitigation when the money runs out.

For the purposes of the argument which follows, then, cinema in Britain means films to be shown, places to project them, and people to see them; at a secondary level it also means a culture of cinema, by which I roughly mean a certain level of discussion of the cinema experience whether in the media or in ordinary conversation and some sort of machinery to support this discussion. British films means in the first instance a certain industrial structure – capital, studios, personnel – producing films for the national and inter-national markets with a principally British investment in British plant, talent and labour; and it also means, or implies, a certain Britishness (however defined) in the resulting product, something which establishes these films as meaningfully British – and not just 'made in Britain' because Britain was a convenient place to make them in.

These different aspects – film-making and cinemagoing, econ-omics and culture – do not in practice exist in isolation from each other, but it is worth making the effort to imagine that they might, since such a scenario is by no means utterly unreal. It is not inconceivable that there should still be cinemagoing in Britain, but that the films gone to would be entirely foreign. Even in the 1940s and 50s, when there was still a sizeable British film industry, most of the box office was for American films. The situation is not dissimilar today, except that (as we shall see) the boundary between 'British' and 'American' is less fixed. The surviving British compo-nent could disappear as an identifiable entity, and all films screened could be American (or Brito-American with the odd sprinkling of

Australian or French or Indian), but there would still be a cinema – of a kind.

Similarly, one can in theory envisage a cinema in Britain shorn of most of its cultural aspects. A bit like Bingo. This is implausible, since every leisure activity – snooker, motor sport, tapestry weaving – generates or is supported by a culture, as a visit to any newsagent will confirm. But it is not impossible, and it is also not impossible for there to be a film culture connected with very little cinema-going; people buy books on Westerns, but hardly any new Westerns are being made, and the old ones are mostly to be seen on TV, not in the cinema.

British films, too, could survive without a cinema. The industry could be busy making films suitable to be shown in cinemas, but they could in fact only ever be shown in Britain on the small screen, and be cinematically projected only at festivals or on release in other markets where cinema was still a going concern. Furthermore the films could be wholly or partly British in an industrial sense without any national-cultural component at all; they would just happen to have been manufactured in Britain in the way that some Ford Escorts happen to have been manufactured there.

In practice, of course, the elements remain interdependent. British films need and have a certain home market; they also remain part of national culture. For its part, cinemagoing still seems to require a national component; the cinema is not yet a place of exile. But an awareness has developed, both in the industry and outside (in the 'culture', one might say), that this interdependence can no longer be taken for granted. A fragmentation has taken place, and a serious question has arisen of how far it can be allowed to go. Is it completely inevitable that the elements will continue to drift apart? Or can they, should they, be held together, and to what degree? Behind the vapid sloganising about 'British films on British screens' (tacky films on tatty screens?) stand some hard calculations about the size of the necessary home market, the strength of the infra-structure, the role of seemingly uneconomic cultural activities in maintaining the cinema as a force in popular life. Although the terms of the cinema equation are fixed, the proportions in which they are combined can and do vary and are likely to change even more dramatically in the years ahead.

The main external variable responsible for changes in the equa-tion is, of course the new technologies, of which television was the first in time and is still the first in importance. Already a situation exists where more film viewing takes place in front of TV screens than ever took place in cinemas, even in the peak post-war years. (Admittedly much home viewing is far less attentive and far less of an experience than cinemagoing and cinema watching: hence the use of the anodyne word 'viewing' to describe it.) The proportion of British films seen on broadcast TV or video is low, reflecting in the first instance the historic dominance that Hollywood has always had in cinema and film-making but also no doubt the fact that broadcast television is protectionist and the TV schedules contain a rather higher proportion of British material made specifically for television. None the less a number of gaps in the schedules (particularly on Channel 4) are filled by old British films, with the intriguing result that the history of British cinema is now far more accessible than it used to be. Television also shows more recent British films, thereby covering the function that used to be performed by second-run cinemas and (long ago) by Sunday programmes. The effect of this 'competition' is put an even tighter squeeze on the remaining second-run cinemas and – very important from the producers' point of view – to put a premium on first-run cinema showings as the only occasion on which films can make money from cinematic release.

The most serious problem facing British cinema, however, remains the abiding cultural dominance of Hollywood (a subsidiary but important aspect of generalised American hegemony). Half way through the last century, the Italian writer Ruggero Bonghi embarrassed his compatriots by asking the question: Why is Italian literature not popular in Italy? This question was taken up and treated in more depth by Antonio Gramsci in the 1930s. It is also a question that can pertinently be asked of British cinema in Britain.

Gramsci's answer to the question about the unpopularity of Italian literature (much read by the *cognoscenti* in other countries but hardly at all by the public at home) focused on its ideological deficiencies and its generally retarded character by comparison with the French. It was elitist; when it attempted to be popular it was merely folksy; and it caught nothing of the democratic spirit which informed its French counterparts in the popular field.

Similar criticisms can be levelled, historically, at British cinema which, like Italian literature in Italy, has never been truly popular in Britain. The hidden history of cinema in British culture, and in popular culture in particular, has been the history of American films popular with the British public. The strength of American cinema was never just economic, and cannot simply be attributed to the lower cost of American product offered for export. Certainly economic strategies aimed at capturing the market played their part, but the basic reason for Hollywood's dominance was artistic and cultural. The American cinema set out in the first place to be popular in America, where it served an extremely diverse and largely immigrant public. What made it popular at home also helped to make it popular abroad. The ideology of the American cinema has tended to be far more democratic than that of the cinema of other countries. This in part reflects the actual openness of American society, but it is above all a rhetorical strategy to convince the audience of the virtues and pleasures of being American. Translated into the export arena, this meant a projection of America as intensely – if distantly – appealing. When matched against American films of the same period, their British counterparts come across all too often as restrictive and stifling, subservient to middle-class artistic models and to middle- and upper-class values. Even American society comedies were made for the American masses: their British equivalents, whatever their makers' hopes, were not just about but *for* the upper class and were therefore esoteric to their main potential audience. When the British cinema has attempted to break out of this restrictive mould, it has tended to produce merely an inverted image, rather than a transformation, of traditional values.

To say this is not to argue that the British cinema has always been awful and is destined always to remain so. On the contrary, it is historically an extremely rich and critically under-rated cinema. It is also changing. But it has had certain specific limitations, the effect of which has been to facilitate an American hegemony which, once established, cannot easily be shaken off. And, whatever it may do in the future, the British cinema is in the invidious position of having to compete with an American cinema which, paradoxical as this may seem, is by now far more deeply rooted in British cultural life than is the native product.

If there is any comfort to be gained in the present situation, it lies in a recognition that the old battles have already been lost and the new ones are being fought on a different – and shifting – terrain. For all the fanfares on behalf of an 'indigenous' cinema, it is clear that a significant section of British film-making has now been cut off from its native soil. British cinema is no longer a national cinema in the traditional sense – the sense in which the Swedish, Hungarian or Brazilian cinemas are national cinemas. British films, at the upper end of the market, are international films – in terms of finance, personnel, content, market appeal. In the international market they compete on their own behalf, as films rather than as exemplars of an integrated national production system. The 'British' label attached to a number of recent successful movies conceals a variety of inputs and characteristics. Front-money, end-money, conception, entrepreneurship, stars, technical expertise, studio, location, setting, relation to previous tradition – from film to film any of these may be British while others are not. *Chariots of Fire, The French Lieutenant's Woman, Gandhi, Superman, The Killing Fields*, all in different ways (but none one hundred per cent) lay legitimate claim to being British films, alongside the more obviously domestic *Local Hero* or *A Private Function*. But *Chariots* was not British-financed. *The French Lieutenant's Woman*, adapted by a British playwright for a British (Czech-born) director from a British novel, is a largely American production whose most bankable star at the time of making was the American Meryl Streep. *The Killing Fields* is a British film, but its concern is with the affairs of other countries (Cambodia, the United States, China, Vietnam, ultimately France: a post-colonial scenario in which, for once, Britain was little involved). *Superman* is registered British because of the input of British studios and

Meryl Streep in *The French Lieutenant's Woman*

technicians, but in other respects is all-American. Even *Local Hero*, domestic and provincial though it is, stretches across the Atlantic to Texas, and has American money in it and Burt Lancaster as its only recognised star.

The cinema has always been international, both culturally and economically. It was international because audiences saw films of different national origins. Most of these films, the world over, were American; but the American cinema itself was very cosmopolitan. It was full of emigrés, who had either been lured to Hollywood by the promise of lucrative contracts or had fled there to escape political persecution. And it happily hegemonised the world by setting the action of many films in other countries and cultures (*An American in Paris, Brigadoon, Shanghai Express, The Fall of the Roman Empire*, to give but a few random examples). European cinema, too, has long been devoted to a practice of co-production, particularly within the EEC.

The new free-wheeling internationalism is different. There is less emigration and more jet-setting. Capital crosses frontiers at the touch of a telex. The relations between national industries have been destabilised. A number of recent major films have had no nationality in a meaningful sense at all – *Last Tango in Paris* for example. The effects of the new internationalism on British cinema have been various. On the one hand it has led to the crumbling of the traditional united front in defence of the British film industry between the film unions, the producers' organisations and the intellectual-cultural supporters of the idea of British cinema. Production in Britain is no longer the same as British-originated films; nor does either necessarily have anything to do with British culture for British consumption. What is now defended is often either a sectional interest, or a no longer defensible idea.

But there is no doubt that part at least of the new British cinema has gained enormously from internationalisation (albeit at some cost to strictly national aspirations and definitions). It has become less provincial and less class-bound in its address to its audiences. It has also found ways of surviving in a world where audiences are shrinking everywhere but most of all on the home market.

The Conservative Government's much-maligned Films Bill has at least the merit of recognising the new realities. It recognises first of all that the idea of a British national film industry has been eroded on two sides. On the one side it is no longer strictly national. And on the other side it is no longer uniquely a film industry, since its current activities and future destiny are indissolubly linked with television and the new technologies. It recognises, too, that if British films are left to sink or swim on the ocean of market forces, some of them will undoubtedly swim. And it recognises that the old policy of milking exhibition (of American films) to support production (supposedly of British films) is no longer viable.

If the general trends of the early 1980s continue for the rest of the decade and if there is no change in Government attitudes, the general future is bleak, but not uniformly so. British films (on a tight or loose definition) will continue to be made, and some will

---

**The film industry no longer stands on its own. It now has to serve different audiences through different media. Cable and DBS will increasingly provide opportunities for all areas of UK production over the next decade; but to take full advantage of this there needs to be a more secure financial and organisational base provided by government.** **Lord Wilson of Rievaulx**

---

thrive. But very few indeed stand much chance of recouping their costs on the home theatrical market alone. Exports and/or a television, cable or video release will in almost all cases be essential. The number of theatrical outlets will continue to shrink. More and more small or medium towns will lose their cinemas, and the cinemas that survive will mostly be city-centre showcases for international films (including some which are all or part British). It would be wrong to discount entirely the possibility of a commercial revival. Better product, better marketing, and above all better programming and exhibition conditions in the cinemas that are left could stem the tide for a while. But there is no way the British cinema can count on more than a temporary reprieve, either for production or exhibition.

The main problem for the much-touted British cinema revival is that the making of and going to British films is not a central part of film culture, let alone audio-visual culture in general. Nor is it economically very significant in the context of the leisure industry as a whole. Even if British, or British-American, films can be individually self-supporting, they first face the problem of competing in a restricted and inflexible theatric market. The prospects for growth are dependent on the ability of British films to seize a larger proportion of the market, but it is problematic how many films the market can support, and how many can be self-supporting

155

within it. If budgets were lower, more films could compete, but low budgets tend to mean a loss of the production values necessary to secure export and video/cable sales. Meanwhile, unless there is more variety in programmes, it is hard to see the market picking up, particularly in the provincial areas where most of the audience has already deserted the cinema.

More important than the size of the market, however, is the question of film culture. Supposing that, with the help of cable, British feature film-making gets the boost it requires to remain economically self-supporting, what cultural role will it then have, what links with other cultural activities, and what sort of autonomous presence in British culture? It has often been observed that British films have traditionally been parasitic on more established art forms – novel, theatre, music-hall. In recent years the parasite has changed its host, and now feeds mostly on television and on music. (Culturally, that is; economically the relationship is mostly the other way round.) It is probably safe to say that when the British go to the cinema, it is to see American film stars or else British musicians and theatre and television actors; additionally a minority go to see films by foreign directors. It is probably also safe to say that the British *cinematic* tradition is best embodied in its technicians, who are also (with certain distinguished exceptions) notoriously conservative.

Meanwhile it is worth noting that a dangerous divide has grown up between the 'commercial' and the 'independent' areas of film-making (and, for that matter, exhibition). The disturbing thing about the abolition of the NFFC is not so much that it has taken money out of the system as that it has removed a central span of the bridge linking small-scale experiment with full-scale commercial production. With the BFI Production Board less and less able to finance experimental feature films, the cinematic routes into feature film-making taken by, for example, Chris Petit and Bill Douglas, are being cut off. Moreover, even if the routes were kept open, the cultural divide separating the world of *Chariots of Fire* from that of the Regional Film Workshops is such that few people seem able to travel them.

It is also, regrettably, the case that Britain's is not a very film-oriented culture at any level. There is neither the intellectual interest that exists in France or Italy nor the deep popular involvement that there is in America. It is instructive in this regard to compare the coverage of Cannes or Venice (or of lesser festivals

156

such as Taormina) in the French or Italian press with the coverage
of London or Edinburgh (not to mention Tyneside) in the press in
Britain. It is also worth comparing the Academy Awards (and their
TV coverage) with their pathetic imitation at the British Academy of
Film and Television Arts.

Nevertheless a cinema culture does exist in Britain. The main
problem with it is that it is very fragmented and, partly for that
reason, lacks visibility. The fragmentation is to some extent ideological, manifesting itself in differences of taste and in different ideas
of what cinema is. But it is also structural, connected with the fact
that so much 'cinema' is now to be found on TV. The whole cultural
complex which constitutes British cinema is far more extensive
than the film industry proper, and opens out on wider horizons
than are visible from Wardour Street.

In the late 1980s, it is film culture rather than the film industry
which merits public attention and concern. For fifty years public
policy (as expressed principally in government legislation) has
taken the direction of measures to shore up the British component
of what was seen in cinemas (and also on TV). The means adopted
have been trade measures (quotas, levies, occasional subsidies),
operating under a cultural cover: the business was worth support-

157

ing because the product was artistic and part of national culture. It is time to do away with this humbug and look more closely at what the national culture is and what part British films, new or old, have to play in it. By its lumpen-monetarist approach to the industry, the Conservative Government has swept away some of the humbug. But the effect will be purely negative if the elimination of an industrial policy for the cinema is not used as an opportunity to promote a cultural policy in its place.

To be any use, a cultural policy for the cinema would need to be far-reaching and would have to encroach into the area of the so-called free but in fact highly manipulated market for films. As such it might be unwelcome to those who control or depend upon the market, including the producers of films. In the long term, however, an approach to the problems of cinema which was not directly oriented to the needs of the industry but based on a wider concept of public benefit could be beneficial to the industry too. The British film 'revival' is extremely precarious. The investors' balance sheets may look healthy at the moment, but there has to be anxiety about the cultural base out of which future audiences and future film-makers will emerge. To hold the audience, and hold it in the cinemas, the audience has to be given reasons for taking films seriously. And films to be taken seriously by audiences (as opposed to films which are taken seriously, perhaps too seriously, by their makers and marketers) are not being produced in profusion. The films of the future may have to be for smaller audiences. The important thing is that they should be for audiences who will care.

## Chapter 1, pp. 3–18

1. For a general survey of European subsidy systems, see Charles Eidsvik, 'The state as movie mogul', *Film Comment*, March/April 1979.
2. Interview with the author, March 1982.
3. See, inter alia, Rachael Low's multi-volume *History of the British Film*, George Allen and Unwin, 1948–1985; George Perry, *The Great British Picture Show from the 90s to the 70s*, Hart-Davis, MacGibbon, 1974; Ernest Betts, *The Film Business: A History of the British Cinema, 1896–1972*, George Allen and Unwin, 1973; Roy Armes, *A Critical History of British Cinema*, Secker and Warburg, 1978.
4. The 1983 estimate by the Office of Population Censuses and Surveys is 56,376,800.
5. The full list can be found in the *BFI Film and Television Yearbook*, 1984, pp. 278–279 (at the time of writing, the latest Films Bill has yet to be enacted).
6. The journalist was David Hewson, writing in *The Times* on 13 April 1983.
7. Mamoun Hassan, 'Britain and the lucky strike syndrome', *Guardian*, 21 April 1983.
8. This is not to imply that all these agencies were set up as a result of the 1957 Act. The CFF dates back to 1951, the NFTS was set up in 1971, and the BFI Production Board in its present form came into being in 1969.
9. Further details of this proposal are contained in the next chapter.

## Chapter 2, pp. 19–30

1. For a fuller and more detailed examination of the backgrounds of the new generation of film-makers, see James Park's *Learning to Dream: The New British Cinema*, Faber, 1984.
2. See Jayne Pilling, 'Exhibition in France: Utopia Unlimited', *Sight & Sound*, 1984.
3. In addition to Matthew Silverstone's analysis in Chapter 3, see Alan Stanbrook, 'The books of the films', *Stills*, July–August 1983.
4. A Workshop may operate under the terms of the Workshop Declaration as and when it is 'enfranchised' by the Union. Essential qualifications include a minimum number of full-time staff, an approved range of activities, a non-profit distributing constitution and receipt of monies only in the form of grants. Outside agencies may not acquire exploitation rights in Workshop Projects where ACTT members have been paid only at rates applicable under the Declaration.

## Chapter 3, pp. 31–42

1. Gail Hegarty Fell, 'The Taxing Question', *Euromoney*, June 1983.

## Chapter 4, pp. 43–56

1. The most notable failures were *Can't Stop the Music* and *Honky Tonk Freeway. Convoy* and *The Jazz Singer* were moderately successful. The last three Spikings films, *Frances, Tender Mercies* and *Cross Creek* represent an interesting switch to 'quality' subjects, but have not proved popular at the box office. *Slayground*, an uninspired Anglo-American thriller, though initiated by Spikings, was made under the auspices of new production head, Verity Lambert.
2. Lorana Sullivan, *Sunday Telegraph*, 3 February 1980.
3. For the *Gossip* story see 'A Cautionary Tale', *AIP & Co.*, August 1983 and 'Martini on the Rocks', *Private Eye*, 30 December 1983. In February 1985, Boyd formed Tartan Films with Hamish McAlpine and Alan Kean, founder of ITC Film Distributors. The company will distribute as well as produce films.
4. Interview Denis O'Brien, Ray Cooper, George Harrison, May 1983.
5. *AIP & Co.*, June 1980.
6. *Screen International*, 19 July 1980.
7. *Glasgow Herald*, 16 August 1982.

Unattributed background material comes from interviews with Jake Eberts and Sandy Lieberson, Don Boyd, and Denis O'Brien, Ray Cooper and George Harrison of HandMade.

## Chapter 5, pp. 57–70

1. Christopher Wicking and Tise Vahimagi, *The American Vein*, Talisman, 1978.
2. Prix Italia for 'Made in Britain' 1984.

## Chapter 7, pp. 83–98

1. *An Introductory Discussion Paper from the Organising Committee.*
2. IDEA was formed in 1983 and comprised membership of both grant-aided and independent commercial distributors and exhibitors. Potentially of enormous political strength and value, IDEA suffered in the same way as the IFA, since without funds or even a part-time organiser, its effectivity was bound to be limited and eventually it was wound up in 1984.
3. *Independent Cinema?*, West Midlands Arts, 1978.
4. *Independent Cinema and Regional Film Culture*: Report of the 1980 British Film Institute Regional Conference. University of London Institute of Education, 1981.
5. Although not an independent distributor in the sense of which I am writing here, the Concord Film Library has a remarkable range of material in distribution much of a directly political and/or ideological nature, including for example *Home on the Range*, an extraordinary exposé of the CIA backed nuclear bases in Australia.

## Chapter 8, pp. 99–110

1. *Screen International* No. 338, 10 April 1982.
2. Ibid, No. 247, 28 June 1980.
3. *Marxism Today*, February 1982.
4. Transmitted 27 May 1983.
5. *Standard*, 26 May 1983.
6. *The Times*, 27 May 1983.
7. *Sight and Sound*, Vol. 52, No. 4, Autumn 1983.
8. *Standard*, loc. cit.
9. Geoffrey Nowell-Smith, 'Radio On', *Screen*, Vol. 20, No. 3/4, Winter 1979/80.

## Chapter 9, pp. 111–122

1. David Kehr, 'A Star is Made', *Film Comment*, January/February 1979.
2. Edgar Morin, *The Stars*, translated by Richard Howard, Grove Press, 1960.
3. Freda Bruce Lockhart, 'Stars without a System', *Film Weekly*, 9 April 1938.
4. John Ellis, *Visible Fictions*, Routledge and Kegan Paul, 1982.
5. Bruce Cook, 'Why TV Stars Don't Become Movie Stars', *American Film*, June 1976.

## Chapter 10, pp. 123–138

1. Reviews used are by: John Coleman, *New Statesman* (16 March 1984); Phillip Bergson, *What's On* (15 March 1984); Patrick Gibbs, *Daily Telegraph* (9 March 1984); Philip French, *Observer* (11 March 1984); Iain Johnstone, *Sunday Times* (11 March 1984); Alexander Walker, *Standard* (8 March 1984); Ian Christie, *Daily Express* (9 March 1984); Nigel Andrews, *Financial Times* (9 March 1984); David Robinson, *The Times* (9 March 1984); Arthur Thirkell, *Daily Mirror* (9 March 1984); Margaret Hinxman, *Daily Mail* (9 March 1984); Derek Malcolm, *Guardian* (8 March 1984). Quotes have not been attributed to individuals since it is the institution of reviewing which is at stake here. Because they were on the BFI's microfiche, *New Statesman* and *What's On* have been included, although they are not of course newspapers.
2. Reviews used: Iain Johnstone, *Sunday Times* (18 March 1984); Philip French, *Observer* (11 March 1984); Alexander Walker, *Standard* (8 March 1984); Nigel Andrews, *Financial Times* (9 March 1984); David Robinson, *The Times* (9 March 1984).
3. Seasons at the time this article was written had been by Alexander Walker, Dilys Powell, Derek Malcolm, Nigel Andrews; the quotations below are from those critics writing in the NFT Programme Booklet.

# Index

163